LAY MINISTRY
IN THE
CATHOLIC
CHURCH

Lay Ministry in the Catholic Church

Visioning Church Ministry Through the Wisdom of the Past

A Symposium With Sr. Carolyn Osiek, R.S.C.J.,
Dr. Francine Cardman, Rev. Kenan Osborne, O.F.M.,
Dr. Richard Gaillardetz, Rev. Thomas F. O'Meara, O.P.,
Rev. Michael J. Himes

Editor: Richard W. Miller II

Liguori

LIGUORI, MISSOURI

Imprimi Potest:
Richard Thibodeau, C.Ss.R.
Provincial, Denver Province
The Redemptorists

ISBN 0-7648–1240-8
Library of Congress Catalog Card Number: 2004115600

Scripture quotations are from the *New Revised Standard Version of the Bible,* © 1989 by the Division of Christian Education of the National Council of Churches of Christ in the USA. Used with permission. All rights reserved.

To order, call 1-800-325-9521
www.liguori.org

Contents

Introduction

Richard W. Miller II, Ph.D. Candidate in Theology, Boston College

I would like to begin today's symposium with some introductory remarks on both the format and subject matter of this conference. First, let me turn to the format.

In his book *A People Adrift: The Crisis of the Roman Catholic Church in America*, Peter Steinfels maintains that "today the Roman Catholic Church in the United States is on the verge of either an irreversible decline or a thoroughgoing transformation."[1] Whether one agrees or disagrees with Steinfels' assessment, one would have to recognize that these are challenging times for the Church. This lecture series was inaugurated to provide a forum for reflection and conversation on central issues facing the Church today. While there are other lecture series that emerged out of the sex abuse scandal, this lecture series is distinctive in its insistence that all reflection on the future direction of the Church must be thoroughly grounded in Church history and historical theology.

Why is it so important to ground all discussion in the history of the Church? Not only is it significant for the present community to recognize the ways in which the Church has developed and changed in two thousand years so that we can draw upon our rich history to face the challenges of today, but also and even more basically, it is central that we as a community come to grips with the fact that the Church has changed.

Many Catholics still refuse to acknowledge that the Church has changed and developed. How many times have we heard Catholics, from the ordinary believer in the pew to those in positions of lead-

---

1. Peter Steinfels, *A People Adrift: The Crisis of the Roman Catholic Church in America* (New York: Simon & Schuster, 2003), 1.

ership, say in one way or another that the Church in its teaching, preaching, patterns of living, and forms of worship has not changed or developed?

This tendency to see the Church as an immutable institution that is beyond time and change is especially tempting in challenging times like these. It is tempting to condemn the present age with all its uncertainty and imaginatively return to an untroubled golden age when the Church was above the messiness and chaos of the world, where the institutional Church was guided unerringly by the Holy Spirit and was free of corruption and the trappings of power, an age where moral norms and boundaries were clearly established and accepted as inviolable, where the truth was clear and never changing, an age when all was light without shadow.

This temptation to immortalize a particular age or epoch as the one true and absolute expression of the faith is a temptation in the full religious sense of temptation. It is a temptation to unbelief and idolatry.

Hidden in the desire to return to a golden age is the temptation to lose faith and trust that the Spirit of Christ is present here and now working through all things, drawing all things through Christ to the Father.

The temptation to idolatry also lurks in this imaginative return to the so-called good old days. The first commandment admonishes us not to make for ourselves an idol, "whether in the form of anything that is in heaven above, or that is on the earth beneath" (Exodus 20:4). The prohibition against idolatry warns us that every form, pattern, or particular way of living out our Christian faith is limited and finite. While particular patterns or forms of living out our faith point to the presence of God in our midst, they do not exhaust the ways God is manifested to us. God is not reined in or captured by our finite means of expressing our faith, for the Holy Spirit blows as it wills (John 3:8). To in any way suggest that a particular time, including our own, perfectly embodies the Spirit of God is to make something finite infinite, to make something relative absolute. It is to fall into idolatry.

John's Gospel tells us that the truth will set us free (8:32). The truth that the Church has changed and developed from the age of the New Testament through the age of the Second Vatican Council is particularly liberating for the present community: If it were true that the Church has not changed and cannot change, we would be unable to take the necessary steps to face the challenges of today so that the Church can flourish in its preaching, teaching, and sacramental ministries.

Now let me turn our attention to the subject matter for today's conference; namely, lay ministry. In the past thirty years there has been a tremendous growth in the number of lay ministers. As of 1999, there were nearly 8,000 more lay ministers than active diocesan priests.[2] Eighty percent of these lay ministers were women, of whom fifty-five percent were nonreligious.[3] In addition, the number of formation programs to train people for lay ecclesial ministry increased by 50 percent from 1986 to 1999, and the number of participants grew by 300 percent.[4] As of 1999, over 31,000 people were enrolled in lay-ministry formation programs, while only 1,868 men were in seminaries preparing to become priests.[5]

A central factor in the growth in lay ministry is obviously the shortage of priests. In the United States, from 1965-2003, there was

---

2. There were over 30,000 lay ministers as of 1999 and 22,394 active diocesan priests. Center for Applied Research in the Apostolate (CARA), *Catholicism USA: A Portrait of the Catholic Church in the United States*, eds. Bryan T. Froehle and Mary L. Gautier (Maryknoll, NY: Orbis Books, 2000), 154, 113.

3. Ibid., 154.

4. Ibid., 160. In 1985-1986, there were 206 lay-ministry formation programs with 10,500 participants; by 1999-2000, 331 lay-ministry formation programs with 31,168 participants.

5. Ibid., 160, 118.

a 65 percent decrease in the ratio of the number of priests to the total number of Catholics.[6] Consequently, as of 2003, one of every six parishes in the United States did not have a resident priest.[7] Moreover, due to the aging of the clergy, the priest shortage in the United States in the next ten to fifteen years will get dramatically worse. As of 1999, nearly one of every four priests in the Church in the United States was retired, sick, or otherwise not actively engaged in full-time pastoral ministry.[8] The average age of diocesan priests active in ministry in 1999 was fifty-nine years, with 15 percent of diocesan priests over seventy-four, 22 percent from sixty-five to seventy-four, and another 22 percent from fifty-five and sixty-four.[9] This means that in five years there will be at least a further 20 percent decrease in the number of active diocesan priests.

While it is certainly true that the tremendous growth in the number of lay ministers in this country can be understood as a response to the declining number of priests, there are also theological reasons for this growth in lay ministry. The Second Vatican Council's Decree On the Apostolate of Lay People (*Apostolicam Actuositatem*) maintained that the "lay people, too, sharing in the priestly, prophetical and kingly office of Christ" and thus "play their part in the mission of the whole people of God" (AA 2). The foundation for this lay apostolate, according to *Apostolicam Actuositatem,* is the Lord himself:

---

6. Calculated from data provided by the Center for Applied Research in the Apostolate (CARA), "Frequently Requested Church Statistics" at http://cara.georgetown.edu/bulletin/index.htm. (Washington, D.C.: Georgetown University, 2004).

7. Ibid.

8. CARA, *Catholicism USA,* 115.

9. Ibid., 112.

Lay people's right and duty to be apostles derives from their union with Christ their head. Inserted as they are in the mystical body of Christ by baptism and strengthened by the power of the holy Spirit in confirmation, it is by the Lord himself that they are assigned to the apostolate (AA 3).

I suggest that, while the declining number of priests has been an important contributing factor in the great increase in the number of lay ministers, it is not the only factor, and it would be a mistake to conclude from this that lay ministry is ultimately about filling in for absent priests. On the contrary, I suggest that the priest shortage is finally forcing us to reflect upon and recognize the full significance of lay ministry, which is inherent in what it means to be baptized members of the Catholic community.

In this vein, I would like to conclude my remarks and begin today's conference with the words of Bishop Anthony Pilla, the Bishop of Cleveland, who in 1998 in his final address to the bishops as President of the United States Conference of Catholic Bishops said the following:

I would like to dispose of the idea, often expressed, that this emphasis on the role of the laity is merely pragmatically useful, given the fewer priests in so many areas of our nation. While the laity have certainly helped cope with the situation, the renewal for their role is more than a pragmatic necessity. It springs from an interior renewal of the very meaning of what it is to be Church, in which we are guided by the Holy Spirit who renews the face of the earth.[10]

---

10. CARA, *Catholicism USA*, 152.

1. Who Did What in the Church in the New Testament?

Sr. Carolyn Osiek, R.S.C.J., Brite Divinity School, Texas Christian University

By mutual agreement with Francine Cardman, the next speaker, I am going to go a little beyond the New Testament, through the second century. Even in this short time of a century and a half, we must distinguish several different phases beginning with the time of Jesus. Beyond his time, four more phases must be pointed out. You will not remember all the details, and that is not important; the point is that ministry always evolves. It is always moving and changing and developing organically.

I smiled when Richard Miller talked about looking back to the "good old days"; there is a wonderful quote from the Roman historian Tacitus at the turn of the first century, who said, "In the good old days, women stayed home and took care of their children, and they don't anymore." We all imagine an earlier golden age to which the present cannot measure up.

The first stage of development of ministry, then, is the time of Jesus and the disciples, which of course we can access only through the gospels and other outside information about life in Roman Palestine. This time was characterized by an itinerant preaching and healing ministry—many concentric circles and networks, common meals given extraordinary significance, and occasional forays of disciples in Jesus' name to preach, exorcise, and heal. So ministry at this point was preaching, exorcising, and healing. That is simply the phase of Jesus' own ministry in Jesus' own lifetime.

Beyond that, then, we move into what we could really call the Church and into the first of four phases of development of Church ministry. The first phase is the first generation, which we know mostly from the Pauline churches. The second phase is second and third generation, what we call the post-Pauline churches, as seen in the Deuteropauline literature and other works contemporary with it. The third phase is mid second century, and the fourth phase is late second century. In each case, we can distinguish changes.

It is also helpful to make another distinction for the sake of understanding what we are talking about, a distinction of two different kinds of ministry: a ministry of leadership and a ministry of pastoral care. By no means do I mean to suggest two different groups of people, or clergy and laity, or anything like that. This is simply a way of clarifying what ministry was, and in fact sometimes the same people did both. For instance, the ministry of the prophets certainly had to do with both leadership and pastoral care. So it is simply a way of clarification to better understand.

For the first generation, the first post-Jesus phase in the Pauline generation, about the year 55 of the first century, about twenty to twenty-five years after the death of Jesus, this is the information we get from the Pauline churches.

Small groups of Christians spread out in many different cities, particularly in the eastern Mediterranean, and they met at least once a week in houses or rented rooms. We make a big deal about house-churches; indeed, that is the basic information we get from the Pauline churches, but there are suggestions that in some cases they didn't have a house that really could be appropriate. In that case, they rented a room for the occasion, but they were meeting in a familiar place and predominantly, I think, in private houses.

They met on the Lord's Day, probably around 3:00 or 4:00 in the afternoon, because that was the time when a formal banquet would begin. They would meet for a common meal; Paul called this meal the Lord's Supper. Eventually it took on the name of *Eucharist*, but originally *Eucharist* simply meant *thank you* or prayer of thanksgiving (as it does, for example, in 1 Corinthians 14:16). If they met in a house, the meal was probably led by the host or hostess of the house, the patron of the house, who then was also the patron of the community.

It was first an ordinary meal. At the end there was a special blessing, the words over the bread and cup, and the sharing of the bread and the cup. After this came reading, preaching, and prayer. In other words, the order of Service of the Word and Service of the Altar were the reverse of what we know. The original order, we are pretty sure, was as I have described, because this was the order of the formal banquet: first you ate and then, in an ordinary situation, you started drinking, and once you started drinking came the entertainment and the philosophical discussion. I am not suggesting a lot of drinking here, but that was the order of the banquet. So probably it was first a meal. At the end of the meal was what we call Eucharist, special prayers and sharing of the bread and cup, followed by what we would call the Service of the Word.

There was also, at the same time, a network of visitation and instruction. We know that they did not get together just for this major meal; they also had other times of contact. The house-church—and if they did not meet in a house-church, there was some family or household that was the center of this—became a center for instruction and social services as well. This was where you went for further instruction in the faith. When you were interested in joining, this was where you went to learn the next step. This was where you went when you were in financial need. This was where you went when you had a believer-visitor coming from outside who needed hospitality. This was where you went to seek hospitality when you were a visitor. This was where you went to get the news about what was going on in other churches. How did people learn what it was to be a Christian? By the activities that went on here.

So you see, already ministry of both leadership and pastoral care was happening. There were some designated leaders. We know that Paul in 1 Corinthians 12 says that in the Church, God has established apostles, prophets, and teachers. He even gives an order: first, apostles; second, prophets; third, teachers. Then he lists many other kinds of charisms or spiritual gifts. In 1 Thessalonians 5, he says you should respect those who preside and admonish you. In Romans 16:1-2, Phoebe is both a patron and a *diakonos,* a deacon of the church of Cenchreae. At the beginning of the Letter to the Philippians, Paul addresses the *episkopoi* and *diakonoi.* At Philippi, there were already designated terms for leaders. Probably there the *episkopoi* (I deliberately say the word *episkopoi* rather than translate it because translations of that word are so difficult) were the patrons of the house-churches in Philippi, which by that time had some kind of common organization or network among themselves.

I stress the importance of prophecy as a gift of the Spirit, available to all. It is very interesting that nowhere in the history of the early Church did anyone try to limit prophecy to certain types of people. Prophecy was always understood as a gift of the Spirit, freely given. There are all kinds of problems about discerning true prophecy—that is something we could talk about for the rest of the morning. But once prophecy is discerned, there is never a question of whether only certain kinds of people can do this. Prophecy is both a gift of leadership and of pastoral care because prophets initiate action. In the name of God, they say, "Thus says the Holy Spirit: let us do this." Then everyone must discern whether we should do it. But prophets are also those who come to the aid of suffering people by speaking a word of encouragement in God's name.

Already in this first generation, there was sacrificial language about the death of Jesus and about the Christian life. The beginning of Romans 12 has been called the charter of the Christian life, according to Paul's theology. He says, "present yourselves as a living sacrifice." The death of Christ is already understood to be a sacrifice, and we share in that sacrifice not by participating in an actual sacrifice of incense or slaughter of animals in a temple, as the rest of the people did, but by our daily life. That sacrificial language has a connection to the common meal, as well.

To conclude, in this phase the ministry of leadership was a variety of gifts with some established leadership functions, and pastoral care was done within the context of the house-church, organized largely through hospitality and patronage.

We must stress the importance of patronage in the earliest years because society was structured around it. The powerful protected and nourished others under their care, and it was the kind of society in which if you wanted something, you went to someone powerful and asked for the favor. This arrangement created mutual, but not egalitarian, social bonds. Much work is being done now on how Paul and others of the first generation fit into the patronage system. A considerable amount of ministry was actually done through the patronage system, which means by the individual initiative of well-placed people.

Now let us move to the second and third generations, the second phase, in about 80 to 112, Paul was dead. The first generation was dead. Prophets were still important itinerant leaders. They were still liturgical leaders. We get this information from a text we call the *Didache,* which comes from around this time. We can see a transition happening in this composite text. The prophetic leaders were presumably charismatic in style. Instructions were given about how to do the *Eucharistia,* although prophets could do it the way they wanted. But in a later section of the text, all of this was giving way to a resident leadership of people called *episkopoi* and *diakonoi*—the same terms that were used in Philippians. The understanding is that hands were laid on them with prophecy, as in 2 Timothy 1:6-7; there was also a group of presbyters, but the presbyters were probably the same as the *episkopoi.* There was, most likely, not yet the three-tiered structure of bishop, presbyters, and deacons, but rather two colle-gial groups: *episkopoi* or *presbyteroi* and *diakonoi.*

At this point, second marriages began to be discouraged. Paul had already offered a personal opinion in this direction in 1 Corinthians 7:39-40. We can see that in the list of qualifications for an *episkopos* (1 Timothy 3:1-7). This was, in fact, an egalitarian ap-plication of a Roman ideal of the *univira,* a woman who has only one husband and who does not remarry after divorce or widow-hood. This was an ideal and not often a reality in Roman practice, but that ideal began to be applied to Church leaders with the under-standing that their dedication needed to be solely to the Church. After one marriage, they had fulfilled their obligation to society, and that was enough.

Liturgical traditions were still flexible, but they were beginning to solidify. House-churches and other small units were also orga-nized more on a citywide basis. A collegial body of *episkopoi* or pres-byters (interchangeable terms) were probably the heads or patrons of the house-churches, as with the first stage. Now they were be-coming a bit more recognized. Terminology, though, is still indefi-nite. In Acts 20, Paul gives a speech to the presbyters of Ephesus at Miletus. In the same speech, he calls the same group of leaders *episkopoi, presbyteroi,* and shepherds (*poimaines*) so the terminol-ogy was still fairly loose even at the time that the Acts of the Apostles was written.

In the Shepherd of Hermas, which comes from Rome in this period, there are leaders, presbyters, presiders, and *episkopoi,* and they all seem to be the same people. There was a looking back to the apostolic age, the "good old days," of course. Ephesians 2:20 says the Church is built on the foundation of the apostles and the prophets. There were the beginnings of a need to establish some continuity with the past. So at this point, there was an emphasis in ministry on right teaching, because pluralism and diversity were developing and the ministry of leadership very much began to focus on sound teaching. Church leaders were chosen from the perspective of who held the teaching that really represented the faith of the community. Pastoral care continued, especially through hospitality and patronage. We move now to the third phase. This was mid second century, about 140 or 150. There was a significant change of venue for Christian worship: out of the dining room and into the hall. No longer were groups of Christians meeting in private houses. The buildings may have looked like private houses on the outside, but they were being remodeled on the inside. In buildings that were originally private houses, walls were taken down to create a hall in which a larger group of people could meet. So it was a move from what we call the *domus ecclesiae,* the house-church, to the *aula ecclesiae,* the church hall. The groups were larger, no longer reclining or sitting as at a meal; now they were standing and then sitting on the floor. A text from about this time, the *Didaskalia,* talks about a rectangular hall in which the presiders and leaders of the Church sat in the front, then the men, and then the women in the back; the children could sit anywhere they wanted. The text notes that if someone important came in, you should take care to see that they were seated. But if a poor person came in, you *really* made sure that they had a place. Justin Martyr, in the middle of the second century, talked about a gathering with a presider in this kind of a place. We have the archeological evidence of the house at Dura-Europus, on the Euphrates, way out on the Syrian border, in which exactly this kind of thing was done. The walls of a private house were taken down and a baptistery put in on the other side, so that the house was transformed into this kind of a place for meeting. Now the groups of people were larger. There were bouncers at the door—one of the roles of the deacons and deaconesses, who supervised who came in and whether they were properly dressed.

The beginnings of the three-tiered Church organization can be attributed to Ignatius of Antioch, who died around 110. Ignatius was Bishop of Antioch in Syria, in the East. He was executed as a martyr in Rome. On his way to Rome, as you may know, he wrote letters to various churches. Ignatius seems to have been the proponent of a new form of leadership, which is that of a single *episkopos*— now we can translate this as *bishop*—with a council of presbyters and a group of *diakonoi* (deacons) who assist the bishop. The big puzzle here is, what did the presbyters do? To the best of our knowledge, they were a sort of advisory council. The real leadership was with the bishop and his assistants, the deacons. This form of government had not yet reached Rome, but it was advancing from east to west.

As the triple form of organized leadership in the Church was beginning to catch on, we begin to have language about succession, the idea of a chain of leaders beginning from the earliest times. Each of the major churches was compiling these lists—Antioch did it, Alexandria did it, Rome did it—perhaps because of the increasing pluralism and diversity. They wanted to tie things down and stabilize them, to make sure, "Do we really have the right teaching? How will we know that?" They would know that because their teacher learned it from this teacher who learned it from this teacher who learned it from the apostles. So the ministry of leadership at this time was right teaching based on an authentic understanding of the tradition.

Pastoral care was beginning to be more centralized and no longer merely in the hands of private patrons. Now these patrons, instead of holding dinners for the poor and for widows, instead of going about their own ministry of pastoral care, were encouraged to give money to the Church, which would see to all of these needs. This had already begun at an earlier phase, but it becomes clearer as time moves on. Still, many people were involved in ministry and, not to say that nobody else did anything, but the message spread that a good Christian is someone who contributes to the extent possible to the common fund. Tertullian talks about contributing monthly to a common fund, out of which the Church would help poor orphans, shipwrecked sailors (I have always wondered about that one), old slaves who had been thrown out of the house with no place to go, and all kinds of works of mercy. The kinds of things that at an earlier stage would have been done by individual patrons, the house-church leaders, and the people of wealth and influence were beginning to be more and more a centralized function coordinated by the leadership.

In the fourth phase, late second century, about 180, there was an interesting new initiative called Montanism. It was based on the revival of prophecy. Not as if prophecy was ever lost—I don't think it was; it went through different changes, but I don't think prophecy has ever been lost. I think it is still very much alive but functions in many different ways. The Montanist movement was a charismatic revival that began in Asia Minor and spread, especially to the West. It was very influential in Rome and Carthage. Tertullian became a Montanist in his later years. At first, they were not a separate church— they were the charismatics well within the Church. Only in certain later aspects did they actually separate—were forced out, really— from the main Church. This indicates the great theological pluralism that was happening at this point. For instance, in response to some of this, Tertullian understood a succession of teaching. He challenged the Gnostics—another set of groups in the Church with a different theology—to unfold the list of their bishops, going all the way back to the apostles or apostolic figures. Well, in fact, the Gnostics did do that. They, in fact, had their own line of succession. But Tertullian said, "Theirs isn't as good as ours." So by this time, the need to have a well-established tradition was very important.

In Gaul at about the same time, the theologian Irenaeus answered Gnostic claims of succession by saying the Gnostics could not claim the same level of authenticity. The emphasis here was not on the passing on of power as much as on the succession of right teaching. It was about who had the mind of Christ, who had the understanding of the way it was from the beginning, even though from the beginning there may have been many differences. But the need to establish one's line of authentic teaching was recognized as essential.

The other thing that happened around the same time was the rise of the charismatic authority of the martyrs, something that would really come to the fore in the next century. The understanding was that if you had committed serious sin but could get access to someone who was imprisoned for the faith, you could ask him or her for forgiveness of your sins. If this person was then martyred, your could be sure your sins would be forgiven because the martyr would intercede for you before God, who cannot resist anything a martyr asks. Now that is very interesting, because who else claimed to have authority to forgive sins? The bishop, of course. So there was a tussle between charismatic authority and the established authority in the Church. The time of the martyrs was just beginning at the end of the second century, and the figure of the martyr towered for more than another century as one who has spiritual authority and leadership. There is a gift and a ministry of pastoral care here, as well. This figure of the martyr only gave way in the Constantinian era to the figure of the holy ascetic, the hermit or monk.

Here the ministry of leadership was assurance of right teaching through authorized direct connection with the legitimizing past, even though there were many different networks and different understandings of what that past was. Pastoral care was largely centralized in the work of the deacons and the regular collections for relief of the poor administered by leaders of the Church, although private patronage had not died out and was not completely discouraged. There was greater diversity in the way things operated, as could be expected.

Finally, three points to summarize:

1. There have always been designated leaders, but the forms of leadership evolved flexibly. In the era that I am talking about, no clear understanding of clergy or ordination had developed.

2. The society was hierarchical, a very status-conscious society, much more than any of us know. Power and privilege always have a place, don't they? But in this society, power and privilege were openly recognized. To give everyone their due doesn't mean that everybody gets the same. It means that they get what is due to them, according to their status. Even though this was a very hierarchical and status-conscious society, a healthy tension existed in the Church between designated leadership, charismatic leadership, and private patronage. The function of prophecy and the work of the Spirit were always there. Paul himself recognized this: other than love, prophecy is the highest gift. In 1 Corinthians 14:18-19, he says, "I thank God that I speak in tongues more than all of you; nevertheless, I would rather speak five words with my mind, in order to instruct others also, than ten thousand words in a tongue." Prophecy is the important gift, after love. At the same time, the prophets must prophesy in order. Creative tensions always exist among the movements of the Spirit, the need for order, and the real needs for healing that must be attended to in pastoral care.

3. For the third point, the question is, can we, should we, try to go back to any of these forms, to any of these stages? Probably we can't go back, but we certainly can go forward. When we go forward based on the knowl-

edge of what has been, a freedom is given to us to evolve new forms, new understandings, new interpretations, and new ways of meeting real needs. So knowledge of history is enlightening—to know what has been so we can imagine what will be. But it will never be exactly the same; it will be different.

2. Who Did What in the Church in the First Millennium?

Dr. Francine Cardman, Weston Jesuit School of Theology

Nearly one thousand years of Church and ministry offers both a rich panorama and a daunting prospect. Surveying "who did what in the Church" from the British Isles to the Middle East and from western Europe to Egypt and North Africa over such a time span requires me to delimit the topic and to make some meaningful chronological divisions for considering it. Before I embark on this project, I want to explain several historical and theological presuppositions that have guided my arrangement of this rather whirlwind millennial tour.

My first presupposition is that it is necessary to understand the social and political contexts of the early Church to understand the way in which it came to organize or order its life and mission. Without such historic grounding, our thought and practice of Church and ministry are bound to be historically inadequate and pastorally ineffective.

The second point is that the familiar categories of *laity* and *clergy* are not a useful lens for looking at who did what in ministry during the first millennium of the Church's life. These terms are themselves products of the Church's history, not unchanging givens of Christian experience. As socially constructed concepts that developed and changed over time, they are part of the subject under investigation rather than determinants of what we might find there.

Third, I am convinced that current ecclesiological debates focus entirely too much on matters of juridical prerogatives, exclusionary practices, and categoric, even ontological, distinctions. Focusing on such questions tends to subsume all action and reflection about ministry into narrow categories that do not work for thinking theologically about ministry, ecclesiology, and the future we are called to as Church. Undue concentration on liturgical-sacramental ministries, canonical requirements and restrictions, definitions of what is properly lay or ordained ministry, who is and is not ordained—all this derives from and reinforces the confusion of canonical or juridical developments with doctrine. Doctrine and discipline are too easily equated with divine will and divine law. History will not let us do that. Theology did not dictate the practice of ministry; it was the development of the practice of ministry that gave rise to theological reflection on ministry.

If we focus only on a narrow view of Church and ministry, we forget that ministry exists in and serves the larger context of the Church's mission. We forget to locate mission in the context of baptism and calling. And if we forget those, we also forget that the Church is not about itself but about the proclamation and presence of God's reign. The Church exists for the sake of God's mission to the world: a mission of integral salvation and liberation and a mission of reconciliation and love, both now and in the fullness of God's future. All the Church's ministries and structures are derived from and subordinate to that mission.

Within the sweep of the first millennium—or most of it, given that Professor Osiek's presentation covered the second century as well as the period of the New Testament churches—I will look at four stages in Church history and correlate each with major developments in ministry and mission.[1]

---

1. Justo Gonzalez, *The Story of Christianity*, vol. 1, "The Early Church to the Dawn of the Reformation" (San Francisco: Harper & Row, 1984), is an accessible introduction to Church history in this period. For the history of ministry, Bernard Cooke's *Ministry to Word and Sacraments: History and Theology* (Philadelphia: Fortress Press, 1976) is an exhaustive study. For the history of ordained priesthood and lay ministry in the Roman Catholic Church, Kenan Osborne's *Priesthood: A History of the Ordained Ministry in the Roman Catholic Church* (New York: Paulist Press, 1988) and *Ministry: Lay Ministry in the Roman Catholic Church: Its History and Theology* (New York: Paulist Press, 1993) are invaluable.

The first stage to be considered is the third century and the very beginning of the fourth: a time of imperially directed persecutions and organizational development within and among the churches. Next, the fourth century: the start of the "Constantinian era" saw the consolidation of hierarchical Church structures and offices. The third stage takes a broader view and includes the fifth through the eighth centuries: the disintegration of the Roman empire in the West, the rebuilding of western political and social structures, and new patterns of relationship between the Church, particularly the papacy, and powerful secular rulers.

Finally, the ninth and tenth centuries: "western Christendom," as it came to be known, arose on the foundations laid by Charlemagne.

At each stop on this tour of history, I will ask these questions: Where is ministry located? What kinds of ministries are there? Who is doing what, and why?

1. The Third Century: Local and Regional Churches, Martyrdom, and Persecution

The missionary expansion of Christianity across the Roman world continued in the third century. The growing numbers of Christians had attracted attention from their neighbors and also from local Roman officials at various moments during the second century, leading to limited and isolated persecutions and martyrdom of a small number of believers. But during two major periods, one in the middle of the third century and one at the start of the fourth century, Christians were persecuted at the direction of the reigning Roman emperors. Testifying to and suffering for their faith—either by imprisonment and exile or execution—confessors (the former group) and martyrs exercised a ministry of witness and intercession. Their example had the greatest influence on their fellow Christians, and the Church has honored them through the centuries for their faith and courage. They also stirred some Romans to admiration and, occasionally, conversion.[2]

Local churches were the centers of Christian life and mission; as they expanded, more formal organizational structures continued to evolve. To be a Christian locally was to be in a relationship with other Christian communities and individuals in nearby towns and cities as well as with those from more distant places. Forging wider connections in a communion of local churches is a model of ecclesial relationship in this period. The solid beginnings of decision-making were found in regional councils, which were comparable to what national bishops' conferences are or could be in the Church today.

At the same time, the threefold ministry of bishop, presbyters, and deacons that was becoming the norm at the end of the second century was firmly in place by the middle of the century. The office of deaconess—a limited but nevertheless real liturgical and pastoral role for women—came into being during this period; deaconesses were common in the west probably into the fifth or sixth century and longer in the east, but both the Roman Catholic and Orthodox churches have tended to forget about the history of this office until recently.[3]

---

2. For martyr accounts from this period, see Herbert Musurillo, *The Acts of the Christian Martyrs*, "Oxford Early Christian Texts" (Oxford: Clarendon Press, 1972). *The Passion of Perpetua and Felicitas*, circa 202, is a moving narrative of the experience of two young women martyrs and their companions, including a deacon named Saturus. The central portion of the text is most likely Perpetua's own account, written from prison. Bishop Cyprian of Carthage died a martyr in 258, as did Bishop Stephen of Rome. During the imperial persecutions, enough Christians compromised or denied their faith to pose a disciplinary problem when they sought readmission to communion once the persecution ended. Resolving controversies in regard to these lapsed Christians furthered the development of a practice of penance for serious postbaptismal sins.

3. Roger Gryson, *The Ministry of Women in the Early Church*, trans. Jean Laporte and Mary Louise Hall (Collegeville, MN: The Liturgical Press, 1976), surveys the textual evidence for women's ministries through the sixth century. I discuss the development and decline of these ministries in "Women, Ministry, and Church Order," in *Women and Christian Origins*, ed. Ross Shepard Kraemer and Mary Rose D'Angelo (New York and Oxford: Oxford University Press, 1999), 300-29.

The terms *laity* and *clergy* began to come into use during the third century as ministerial offices were more sharply defined and, with the exception of deaconesses, were formally restricted to men. Yet important ministries of the first two centuries continue to be exercised by those newly designated as laity—widows, virgins, and prophets (male and female). We know that laypeople and clergy were martyrs and confessors—in fact, more laypeople than clergy. We know, too, that laypeople continued to play important roles as teachers and patrons.

Among the teachers were bishops, through whose office the apostolic faith of the community was formally represented and officially handed on. But some of the most prominent teachers of this century were also presbyters and laypeople. And some of these teachers were also martyrs or would-be martyrs. One such was Origen of Alexandria (died circa 250), who in his youth had been so eager to be a martyr that his mother hid his clothes to prevent him from achieving his ambition. Only a presbyter, his theological legacy to the Eastern Church was enormous. Tertullian of Carthage in North Africa (died circa 220), was a layman whose extensive writings shaped Christian Latin vocabulary and theology down to the present. Cyprian of Carthage and Augustine of Hippo were his immediate theological and linguistic heirs. No evidence exists of Tertullian's ordination; his influence was solely the result of his theological cogency and his rhetorical abilities.

Ministries of instruction and example were important, particularly among women and in families and often across several generations; widows and virgins usually performed these ministries. Widows also exercised ministries of prayer, visitation, and pastoral care with other women, especially the sick and the poor, activities that sometimes came into conflict with the newer organization of these ministries under the bishop's leadership and the deacon's services. Patrons, too, both male and female, engaged in ministries of mercy to the poor, orphans, strangers, and the sick; they also came into conflict with the restructuring of the Church's charitable and social services.

Widows appear to have exercised a ministry of prophecy that was a continuation of an older charismatic tradition and the source of some tension in relation to the offices of bishop, presbyter, and deacon. Periodically, this tension would escalate into polemic against the widows, pitting them against the deaconesses, who were usually portrayed as the ecclesial "good girls" in contrast to the "bad girl" widows who needed to be reigned in as structures of ministry became more formal.[4]

The experience of widows and patrons in the third century shows that, even as Church life became more structured and ministry began to be defined around cleric offices, laywomen and laymen continued to engage in a number of traditional, more charismatically based ministries. They did this sometimes inside, sometimes outside, and sometimes in conflict with the movement toward Church order and institutionalization. Such diversity should not be deplored because the tension it generates is a healthy reminder of the ongoing need for all the dimensions of ministry—individual, charismatic, prophetic, and institutional—in the life and mission of the Church.

To summarize, this first period offers a model of ecclesial relationships in which local churches were joined together in a communion with a developing practice of regional decision-making. Structures, styles, and locations of ministry continually evolved. Both lay people and clergy engaged in ministries of witnessing, teaching, leading, and caring. In terms of "who was doing what," both the *who* and the *what* were becoming more clearly and narrowly defined, yet a diversity of gifts and ministries continued to be manifest.

---

4. For tensions between widows and deaconesses, see Cardman, "Women, Ministry, and Church Order," 308-18.

2. The Fourth Century: The Constantinian Era

Constantine, the first Christian Roman emperor (305-337), was baptized only on his deathbed but had a tremendous influence on the shape, direction, and style of the Church over the course of his reign. With the end of persecution and an imperial policy of religious toleration, the Church grew rapidly in the fourth century, becoming socially acceptable and, by the end of the century, the established religion of the empire.

The fourth century is the era of the Christianization of the Roman empire and the imperialization of the Church. If we celebrate the first of these transformations without also acknowledging the second, we distort history and limit our ability to understand the way in which leadership, authority, and power are exercised—not only in the fourth-century Church, but in our own time as well. For the sake of brevity, I will focus mainly on western developments in this period.

The Constantinian era marked a change in the relationship of Church and empire, Church and political powers, that continued into the late middle ages at least. Hierarchical structures were explicitly elaborated and bishops, who were already solidly entrenched as leaders of their Churches, became important political as well as ecclesial figures. Relationships among bishops became hierarchical: although all bishops were thought to be equal and to exercise the ministry and authority of Peter, some bishops were held to be more equal and more Petrine than others. Bishops of important cities in the provinces of the Roman empire, usually the provincial capital or metropolis, were recognized as "metropolitan bishops," something like archbishops today. Bishops of even more important, more ancient, larger cities and churches constituted a rank above the metropolitans. These were the patriarchal bishops—a role played by the bishops of Antioch, Alexandria, Constantinople and, later, Jerusalem in the East, but in the West only by the bishop of Rome. The addition of Constantinople to this list is significant: the Church of Constantinople was important because it was "the new Rome," the imperial capital after 330, and its bishop gained in stature and influence because of his proximity to and inevitable involvement with the imperial court.

This was the period, too, of ecumenical councils, beginning with the Council of Nicaea in 325, when decision-making was meant to apply to the entire Church rather than to regions of culturally and politically related cities and churches or local churches. Although there was a good deal of variation in the acceptance and effectiveness of the decisions and decrees of these ecumenical councils, their form of centralized decision-making became a model for subsequent centuries.

The Church became prominent, even prosperous, under Constantine. Martyrdom gave way to asceticism and monasticism as central expressions of Christian witness.[5] Women and men who undertook lives of asceticism, whether as solitaries or in religious communities, stood in large measure as counterwitnesses to the Church's new social and political arrangements. The ascetic and monastic movements of the fourth century and beyond provided a critique of the ways in which the Church was becoming enculturated and accommodated to its culture.

Patronage was increasingly important in the fourth century, but its exercise went beyond individual relationships within local churches. Patronage was now on a much larger scale: the imperial family and the elite raised shrines to commemorate saints and mar-

---

5. In *Late Antiquity* (Cambridge, MA, and London: The Belknap Press of Harvard University Press, 1998), Peter Brown discusses Church leadership, asceticism, and a new Christian marital morality in relation to the Greco-Roman world and Judaism; this small book reprints his chapters on Christianity from *A History of Private Life*, vol.1: "From Pagan Rome to Byzantium," ed. Paul Veyne, trans. Arthur Goldhammer (The Belknap Press, 1987).

tyrs and built monasteries and endowed episcopal sees and funded their charitable ministries. The newly appreciated or rediscovered holy places in and around Jerusalem attracted pilgrims, and arrangements had to be made to accommodate their desire to see the places of Jesus' life and death and of the biblical stories. Patronage made all this possible, beginning with perhaps the most significant patron of all, Constantine. Wealthy Romans, especially women, were major benefactors, at times competing with or even surpassing bishops in their influence.

Paula, a widow from an aristocratic Roman family, was one such patron. She belonged to a circle of women in Rome who looked to Jerome as their teacher. Ultimately she left Rome and her family and traveled to the holy places of Roman Palestine and Egypt, settling finally in Bethlehem, where she funded the double monasteries for men and women that she and Jerome headed. She prayed and studied the Scriptures, learned Hebrew (she was better at it than he was, Jerome reported), and became an astute exegete, offering solutions to scriptural conundrums that she was too modest to put forward on her own, as Jerome notes, so he included them in his own biblical commentaries. The patronage that Paula offered Jerome went beyond the material needs of their ascetic and scholarly lives and became spiritual and intellectual companionship.[6]

Ministries of mercy—pastoral and material care for refugees (a growing problem in the late-fourth and early-fifth centuries), for those suffering from famine, and for the poor, the sick, and the orphaned or abandoned—were much needed in this period, and patrons made such ministries possible.

---

6. Jerome's Letter 108 to Eustochium recounts Paula's pilgrimage, studies, and asceticism to her daughter; trans. in *Handmaids of the Lord: Holy Women in Late Antiquity and the Early Middle Ages*, ed. and trans. Joan M. Petersen, Cistercian Studies Series 143 (Kalamazoo, MI: Cistercian Publications, 1996), 123-67.

Good examples of ministries undertaken at episcopal direction are the charitable communities formed by Basil the Great, bishop of Caesarea in Cappadocia, to relieve the famine of the 380s, and the insistent preaching of John Chrysostom, bishop of Constantinople in the 390s, who continually urged his congregation to perform works of justice and charity.[7] Chrysostom promoted asceticism and simple lifestyles and was often biting in his critiques of conspicuous consumption and ostentatious displays of wealth. Since he was preaching not only to the general populace but also to the imperial court, it is not difficult to imagine how unpopular he became. He so enraged the empress Eudoxia with some of his homilies that he was finally sent into exile in 404.

The influence of the ascetic-monastic movement on the Church as a whole and on these ministries of mercy is reflected in the fact that both Basil and John Chrysostom were monks before they were bishops, a path that was becoming more common in the later fourth century. Ascetic values inspired many of the patrons of these ministries, and lay people in general were instrumental in the practice and material support of mercy and hospitality.

A third area of ministry that became more prominent in the fourth century was the ministry of teaching, catechesis, and theology. Much of this work was now done by bishops and presbyters, and the last quarter of the century is the age of the great bishop-theologians: Ambrose, Augustine, and Jerome in the West, and Basil the Great, Gregory of Nyssa, and John Chrysostom in the East. At the same time, however, laypeople avidly caught up in the doctrinal debates of the period constituted a critical mass of support for the faith represented by the Nicene Creed.

---

7. See Justo Gonzalez, *Faith and Wealth: A History of Early Christian Ideas on the Origin, Significance, and Use of Money* (San Francisco: Harper & Row, 1990), 173-86 and 200-13, for Basil and John Chrysostom.

Some laypeople stand out as teachers and theologians, one of the most notable being Macrina, sister of Basil and Gregory of Nyssa. Gregory attributes to Macrina the faith, asceticism, and theological wisdom that he and his brother learned in their family; she was, he said, the "teacher of all of us."[8]

Widespread participation in these ministries counterbalanced to some degree the process by which ordained ministries became more sharply delineated in the era of Constantine. Even as Church structure became more hierarchical, both laypeople and clergy continued to participate in the calling and election of their ordained leaders—bishops, especially, but also presbyters and deacons. They were chosen through prayer, popular acclamation, patronage and, at times, imperial pressure. But for the most part they were chosen locally by the communities for which they were ordained, as documents known as Church orders (from the early-third and late-fourth centuries) show.[9]

To summarize, central aspects of Christian life and ministry in the fourth century were the shift from martyrdom to asceticism and monasticism as a prominent mode of spirituality and witness; the hierarchical organization of ordained ministry and episcopacy; public ministries of mercy; and the flourishing of theology, catechesis, teaching, and preaching.

---

8. For Gregory of Nyssa's *Life of Saint Macrina,* see Petersen, *Handmaids of the Lord,* 39-86.

9. The *Apostolic Tradition* of Hippolytus of Rome (circa 212); the *Didascalia Apostolorum* (Teachings of the Apostles) from Syria or Palestine (circa 230); the *Apostolic Constitutions,* a Syrian collection that incorporates these earlier texts and adds a great deal of new material. For an introduction to these documents and bibliography on texts and translations, see Edward Yarnold, "Church Orders," in *The Study of Liturgy,* ed. Cheslyn Jones, Geoffrey Wainwright, Edward Yarnold, and Paul Bradshaw, rev. ed. (New York: Oxford University Press and London: SPCK, 1992), 89-91, as well as other essays on specific topics.

3. Fifth Through Eighth Centuries: Rebuilding the West

Beginning in the late-fourth century, the "barbarian invasions" of the western Roman empire reached crisis points in 410, with the sack of Rome by the Visigoths, and in 451, when the Vandals laid siege to the city and were bought off by Leo the Great (Leo I), the bishop of Rome.

For the most part, however, these "invasions" were more like migrations punctuated by warfare as Germanic peoples from northern and central Europe and central Russia moved across the frontiers of the empire in the West. Some of these peoples were Christians but heretic, having been evangelized by Arian missionaries in the 340s; most were not Christian at all. But all were regarded as alien to Roman civilization and Christian faith and a threat to the mutual interests of Church and empire.

The disintegration and gradual reorganization of the western empire in these centuries is a crucial political and social context for developments in the Church. The growing importance of the Roman bishop owes much to this political process. That he was the only patriarchal bishop in the West—there were four patriarchs in the East—enhanced the claims to a unique apostolic authority of the bishop of Rome, claims that were exercised with increasing effectiveness among western Churches in the centuries to follow.

Another factor in the rising authority of the Roman bishop was the way in which the Roman Church and then other bishops and dioceses used their resources to maintain basic social services and public works during this period of disruption and rebuilding. By the time of Gregory the Great (Gregory I), around 600, the Roman Church was responsible for the bread lines (the welfare system of its day), paying the army, and maintaining the aqueducts. Gregory did this not out of a grasping for power, but out of necessity; joining a sense of public responsibility with Christian values of mercy, he advanced the mission of the Church. Yet the end result was also a great increase in the prestige, influence, and authority of the bishop of Rome in the West.[10]

A point I want to emphasize here—a point too little noticed by Roman Catholics—is that there is not just one "apostolic see" in the early Church. In one sense, all episcopal sees are apostolic, of course. But in terms of sees that were especially recognized for their apostolic authority, authenticity, and antiquity, we have to look to the five patriarchal bishops I mentioned earlier: Antioch, Alexandria, Constantinople, Jerusalem, and Rome.[11]

Turning to other ministries in this period, I want to focus on two areas: one a ministry of mission and evangelization to the new peoples of the western empire and another a ministry of education, already well underway in the fourth century, but taking on new urgency in the changed situation of the western empire and Church.

Mission and evangelization were key activities of this period. The Church began to realize that the Roman empire was over in the West, that the new peoples were there to stay, and that it was time to evangelize the "barbarians" as well as to convert the Arian heretics among them. As in the time of Constantine, the Church again saw its future tied up with secular rulers, in this case the emerging political powers among the new ethnic groups. Two examples show the importance of laypeople, particularly women, in the evangelization of these peoples: one is Clovis and the conversion of the Franks

---

10. For Gregory, see Carole Straw, *Gregory the Great: Perfection in Imperfection* (Berkeley: University of California Press, 1988).

11. For a popular introduction to the history of the papacy and lives of the popes, see Richard P. McBrien, *Lives of the Popes: Pontiffs from St. Peter to John Paul II* (San Francisco: HarperSanFrancisco, 1997); for very detailed information, see *The Papacy: An Encyclopedia*, 3 vols., Philippe Levillain, gen. ed. (New York: Routledge, 2002). I have discussed the question of apostolic sees in "Myth, History, and the Beginnings of the Church," in *Governance, Accountability, and the Future of the Catholic Church*, ed. Francis Oakley and Bruce Russett (New York: Continuum, 2004), 41-3.

in the 490s, and the other is the mission to the British Isles around 600.

Clovis was only fifteen years old when he came to royal power in 381 or 382. His mother served as his regent for a time, and Catholic bishops in nearby territories went to some lengths to convince him that if he took counsel from bishops and followed their advice, God would bless and prosper his kingdom. The bishops saw in Clovis a way to convert not only the Franks, but also the other tribes he would conquer as his kingdom expanded. However, the person most responsible for Clovis' conversion was his wife, Clothilde, who was already a Christian and had her own chaplain. She had their first son baptized against Clovis' will and—not an effective argument for Christianity—the child died. Undaunted, Clothilde had their second son baptized and, fortunately, this child survived. Under continuing pressure to convert, Clovis finally committed himself to Christianity when, in a situation parallel to Constantine's experience at the Milvian Bridge, he asked for the assistance of Clothilde's God in a battle and was victorious. Clovis was instructed in Christian faith and baptized in 496 along with three thousand of his army.[12]

Similarly in the Roman mission to the British Isles a century later, a crucial role was played by the Frankish princess Bertha, wife of the Saxon king Ethelbert of Kent. Ethelbert was converted as much by Bertha's ministrations and persuasions as by the preaching of the monk Augustine (known later as Augustine of Canterbury) and the example of the monks accompanying him, who had been sent by Gregory the Great to convert the Anglo-Saxons in Britain. Ethelbert was impressed by the procession, cross, images, and chants of the missionary monks who met with him—outdoors, because he was

---

12. Accounts of Clovis' conversion and letters from bishops can be found in *Christianity and Paganism, 350-750: The Conversion of Western Europe*, ed. J.N. Hilgarth (Philadelphia: University of Pennsylvania Press, 1986), 72-83.

afraid to confront whatever supernatural powers they might unleash within the confines of a building. In time Ethelbert was baptized, and many in his kingdom followed suit, seeing that he favored Christians as his fellow citizens in the kingdom of heaven.[13]

Education declined in the West with the disruptions of the Germanic migrations and invasions. Catechesis also diminished as large groups of people became Christian en masse. Learning was preserved, especially in some of the monasteries in this period; more basic education took place in diocesan schools attached to the bishop's cathedral and court. In the late-eighth century, Charlemagne sought to reform the Church through a series of regional councils and to renew the cultural life of his reign through monastic schools and a palace school at his own court. The revival of learning he set into motion is sometimes referred to as the Carolingian renaissance. Not only did it raise the religious and moral level of his realm, it also created a measure of cultural unity that allowed Charlemagne to consolidate his power as he conquered neighboring peoples.

If the bishop of Rome emerged as one pole of power at the time of Gregory the Great, it was not long before power gathered around a second, secular pole created by the Frankish kings Pepin and Charlemagne. The "two powers," as they came to be called—sacred and secular, priestly (or papal) and royal—assisted, needed, and used each other throughout the Middle Ages. That was the case with Pepin, who asked for papal support and approval of his plan to depose the last of the line of weak rulers before him. It was also the case with Pope Leo III, who called on Charlemagne to protect him and the territories of the Roman Church from the designs of the Lombard kings in northern Italy and from the schemes of powerful Roman

---

13. The story of Gregory, Augustine, and the British mission is told by the Venerable Bede in his *History of the English Church and People*, books I.23-II.3 (Harmondsworth: Penguin Books, 1955), trans. Leo Shirley-Price.

families. Leo in turn crowned Charlemagne as emperor in the West on Christmas Day 800. And so the subtle and not-so-subtle dance of power continued for centuries.[14]

The death of Charlemagne in 814 marked the end of this era of reorganization in the West. The Frankish hegemony was inherited by Charlemagne's descendants, German kings who held the title of Holy Roman Emperor. Mission and evangelization were highly successful, educational endeavors continued in monasteries and in episcopal schools, and the foundations of "Western Christendom" was set.

4. The Ninth and Tenth Centuries: The Rise of Western Christendom

The new political and social order that emerged was feudalism, a society in which politics, economics, and power were rooted in landholding and agriculture. Feudal society was hierarchically structured in an intricate system of relationships in which people owed loyalty and service, including military service, to those immediately above them and were due the same from those immediately below them. Bishops and abbots were an integral part of that structure, since their dioceses, monasteries, and offices were supported by the lands they held. As feudal lords, they owed fealty to the secular princes, kings, and emperors. One small symbol of the Church's insertion into this system can still be found in the ordination rite, in which the ordinand places his hands, palms together in an attitude of prayer, between the hands of the bishop and vows obedience to him. This is the gesture of feudal vassalage, of a knight to his lord or a lord to his king.

---

14. See Brian Tierney, *The Crisis of Church and State, 1050-1300,* "Medieval Academy Reprints for Teaching 21" (Toronto: University of Toronto Press, 1988), 16-23, for documents relating to Pepin, Charlemagne, and the papacy.

Time does not permit me to discuss this last period at any length, so I will simply highlight one of its most important features, the activity of patronage. The relationship between the pope and the Frankish and German kings outlined earlier is a prime example of the interaction of spiritual and political patronage of this period.

A second kind of patronage was found in the power and protection of the saints, their shrines, and their relics.[15] The power that the cult of saints, relics, and pilgrimages to their shrines exercised is fascinating in itself, but even more fascinating, perhaps, is the power struggle that this cult set in motion. Bishops and their churches had collections of relics; abbots and abbesses and their monasteries had relics; kings and powerful lords had the same. Who controlled this spiritual patronage and the authority and income that it generated was an ongoing point of contention. Maintenance of these collections as well as saints' shrines and pilgrimage routes was in itself an act of patronage on the part of ecclesiastical and royal officials. Making such spiritual resources accessible to more ordinary Christians was also a kind of ministry, regardless of who performed it.

A third kind of patronage was the endowment of churches and chapels on the domains of feudal lords ("private churches"), in the first instance to pray for the souls of the family's dead, but also to provide the sacraments to the those who labored on the lands. Patrons also founded and endowed monasteries or left them property in their wills. Farsighted donors such as Duke William of Aquitaine, who built and endowed the monastery of Cluny in 910, were able to institute reforms through their patronage. In the case of Cluny, William stipulated that the abbey should be free of all lay and episcopal

---

15. For saints as patrons, see Peter Brown, *The Cult of the Saints: Its Rise and Function in Latin Christianity* (Chicago: University of Chicago Press, 1981). For a vivid description of the early Middle Ages and the importance of relic collections, see R.W. Southern, *Western Society and the Church in the Middle Ages*, Pelican History of the Church 2 (Harmondsworth: Penguin Books, 1970), 27-33.

control, subject only to the pope, and that even William himself should maintain a respectful distance; the monks were to elect their own abbot without interference. Cluny was one current of reform among others in the tenth century that, taken together, would lead to wider reform of the papacy and the Church in the next century.

Conclusion

I want to make two sets of observations: The first involves the relationship of the Church to the social and political order in which it lives and the implications this relationship has for ministries and other roles in the Church. Integration of the Church into the structures of the Roman empire and then into the reorganized structures of feudalism and Christendom in the West was unavoidable. The Church influences the culture in which it exists, certainly, but also and necessarily is influenced by that culture. It is naive to pretend otherwise and dangerous to ignore the ways in which power relationships are reproduced within the Church, both for good and for ill. From the fourth century onward, the Church and its hierarchy have been dependent on the toleration, favor and, often enough, protection of emperors and kings, yet the balance of power between secular rulers and bishops and popes has continually shifted. If medieval monarchies once provided models for structure, ministry, and governance in the Church, there is no reason that more modern forms of social and political organization—representative democracies, for instance—should not do so in our own day.

The second set of concluding observations involves the role of laity in the ministry and leadership of the Church. Throughout the second through the tenth centuries, laity and clergy participated in the calling and election of their ordained leaders. These leaders came from within a particular community and sometimes from outside it; sometimes they were chosen by popular acclamation, occasionally even against their will; sometimes their selection was determined by powerful secular interests, including emperors; and at other times they were chosen by patrons who funded a Church on their feudal domains or endowed a monastery and wanted to select its abbot or abbess. These processes sometimes went awry, but so have the more centralized processes of recent centuries. It remains that we have a long history, a thousand years and more, of widespread participation of laity and clergy in the calling of Church leaders, especially bishops. Again, there is no reason not to have such participation today.

Finally, this tour of the first millennium highlights the crucial role of laypeople in each period, both the spiritually powerful and the politically and materially powerful. Throughout this period, laypeople have been engaged in activities that must be recognized as ministry: witnessing to Christian faith, evangelizing, and extending mercy. Once the distinction between laity and clergy is no longer seen as determinative of what ministry is or who does it, we will be able to affirm that these ministries of laypeople are as important for the life and mission of the Church as are ordained, sacramental ministries.

3. Who Did What in the Church in the Second Millennium?

Rev. Kenan Osborne, O.F.M., Franciscan School of Theology

In this brief and wide-brush overview of a thousand years of Catholic Church history, I want to consider each century carefully, but generally, beginning with the end of the first millennium, 1000, down through the second millennium, to the year 2000. The focus of my essay is the western Roman Catholic Church; for each century, I will highlight key Roman Catholic figures, major leaders whose influence has continued through the following centuries. Since not every figure or event can be included, my selection focuses in a particular way on laymen and laywomen who were highly influential during their respective centuries.

My goal is to indicate two things: on the one hand, there was throughout the second millennium a growing lay leadership within the Roman Catholic Church; on the other hand, there was a counter-effort during each century to curtail the influence of lay leadership. Nonetheless, when one considers the small beginnings of lay leadership at the year 1000 with the extensive lay leadership at the year 2000, one cannot be but amazed at the steady growth of the laywoman and layman within Church structures. Such growth does not happen by accident. Major theological issues that center on what we call today a theology of Church, an ecclesiology, are involved. Consequently, as we view each century and the steps taken in it toward a great lay presence in the Church itself, I will also point out key factors that took place regarding a theology of Church.

1000

MAIN EVENT	MAIN LEADERS
Beginning of the medieval reform movements	The majority of the first leaders of these medieval reform movements were laymen and laywomen

In the first century of the second millennium (1000 to 1100), a "reform movement" began that had a major influence on the next thousand years. This movement began in a fairly quiet way, with laymen and laywomen gathering in their homes to read and pray over certain biblical passages. As time went by, these groups formed loosely organized lay spiritual communities. In time, some of the lay leaders became better organizers and made their respective movements better known. The growth of these initial lay reform movements was phenomenal. We find such movements in Mainz (1012), Orléans (1022), Arras (1025), and Goslar (1051).

These laymen and laywomen had a very strong "felt need." They were looking for a deeper spirituality, and obviously the clerical leadership at that time did not provide them with the spiritual guidance they wanted. These men and women did not have Bibles; this was before the printing press, and hand-copied Bibles were far too expensive. What they did have were pages called *florilegia*, a readable bouquet of flowers: *flora* = *flowers; legia* = from *legere, to read.* These florilegia contained scriptural passages (mostly from the New Testament) on a given theme such as faith, love of neighbor, prayer, etc. People could not afford to buy an expensive, hand-copied book of several hundred pages, but they could afford a few pages.

Today we might call these "faith-sharing groups," for that is more or less what the people were about. They gathered together, someone read aloud the passages of Scripture, and then the group shared what they "had heard" and what the passages meant for their own spiritual lives and devotion.

The reading of Scriptures, particularly the gospels, began to inspire certain religious—men and women—to rethink the religious life and compare it with the gospel or *the evangelical life.* A number of these monks and nuns became part of the reform movement. They wanted to be part of a religious community in which they could live the evangelical life in a more scriptural way. For instance, the Cistercian reform of the Benedictine Order took place when Robert of Molesmes, a monk (1028-1112), left Molesmes and founded a reform group at Cîteaux. Another instance took place when Bruno of Cologne (died 1101), a diocesan priest, began an evangelical contemplative order known as the Carthusians.

In this same century, Pope Gregory VII (1073-1085) realized that Church reform was necessary. The steps he took are now known as Gregorian reform. The Holy Roman Emperor, Henry IV, also began reform movements, particularly in the Germanic area of Europe. Neither of these "official" reform movements succeeded. For Gregory, reform essentially involved an acceptance of the papacy over and against the emperor. In other words, there was a political dimension to Gregory's reform; if groups did not go along with his political interests, he did not support them. His theology of Church, which was overbearingly institutional, was the major reason the Gregorian reform did not succeed. In Henry's case, the political elements in his theology of Church prevented his own efforts at reform from long-lasting success.

However, the lay movements for reform and some of the monastic movements for reform stayed for the most part clear of political and institutional centering and remained influential. The theology of Church found in these lay movements centered the Church on a spiritual rather than a political or institutional dimension, which is why these movements continued to have an influence, whereas the efforts of Gregory and Henry did not succeed.

1100

MAIN EVENT	MAIN LEADERS
Church hierarchy began to feel threatened by the lay movements	Peter Abelard, a monk, the dominant theologian
	Peter Waldo, a lay preacher
	Hildegard of Bingen
	Elizabeth of Schönau

From 1100 to 1200, reform movements continued at all levels of the Roman Catholic Church, but the hierarchy (popes and bishops) began to feel that laymen and laywomen were encroaching on the institutional boundaries of the Church. There were at first sporadic efforts to control the oversight of these new communities. One way which the hierarchy used to control such lay movements was to call them " heretical." We see this in the reaction of the church hierarchy to the groups called the Cathars and Albigensians. Some of the lay spiritual groups of the period can truly be considered heretical, but Church leadership also used the labels Cathar and Albigensian to discredit groups that were not. The "heretic" label has lasted a thousand years even though only a few of these lay reform movements eventually and officially became "heretical": even in 2004, Church historians refer to them as "heretical reform groups."

One thing the formation of these groups indicates is that a spiritual vacuum existed in the Church of this period, particularly for the spiritual life of laypeople. The hierarchy did not provide the leadership necessary to remedy the situation, so laypeople tried to do it themselves. This was the situation of Peter Waldo and the Waldensians.

A series of quite different events that clearly changed the entire second millennium had begun to take place, beginning with the rediscovery in the West of the writings on Aristotle. From 1100 on, Latin translations of Aristotle's writings made their way into the newly established European universities. In addition, several commentaries by various Arab scholars, also translated into Latin, became part of the university scene. Two Arab scholars in particular, Averroes and Avicenna, were important. In the faculty of arts at the European universities, Aristotle and Arab commentaries became very popular. Laymen were able to attend the faculty of arts, but could not register in the faculties of theology because theology was reserved for clerics. Still, the presence of laymen at the growing universities indicated that education of laymen—and to some degree laywomen—had moved upward in a fast and radical way. More and more people were interested in a deeper spiritual life; in addition, a growing number of laymen and laywomen were highly educated, and education invariably leads to leadership. The result was that a theology of Church (ecclesiology) was beginning to develop that included both educated and spiritually well-developed lay leaders. Both factors eventually led to a challenge of the clerical leadership in the Church. This was evident in a very strong way through the influence of women such as Hildegard of Bingen (1098-1179) and Elizabeth of Schönau (1129-1164), both of whom were well educated and very deeply developed spiritually.

A third factor developed just at the end of this century, namely the beginning of the crusades, with Urban II proclaiming the first crusade at Clermont in 1095. The crusades produced a military leadership that was primarily lay, but they also produced religious military groups that eventually controlled both land and finances. These groups were spiritual because they were religious communities, and they were powerful because of the money and land they controlled.

The crusades provided a new way of being a Christian and of saving one's soul. Urban II mentioned this in his speech at Clermont. A young man would save his soul by taking part in the crusade. This meant that salvation of one's soul did not require a person to become either part of the clergy or part of a religious community. A knight could save his soul simply by being a knight. This did not mean dying in battle. This meant, rather, that the very dedication to regaining the holy places for the Church was "meritorious" for heaven. Again, the status of the layperson in the Church was increased in no small measure. Lay spirituality was endorsed.

1200

MAIN EVENT	MAIN LEADERS
Fourth Council of Lateran (1215)	Saint Francis of Assisi
	Saint Clare of Assisi
	Saint Thomas Aquinas

The Fourth Lateran Council was a major event in the thirteenth century. Almost every leading king, prince, and lord was present, as were almost all major bishops and abbots. The council was a gathering of the elite leadership from all parts of the European world. Many major leaders of the Eastern Catholic Church were present as well. Pope Innocent III must have looked at the gathering in the Lateran Church and gasped in amazement. All of the top people had come to the council he had called. It was a major moment. There were only three sessions, and the entire council lasted only two weeks.

In this short period of time, many issues were accomplished: Joachim of Fiore, the Cathars, and the Waldensians were all condemned. It was decided that all Western Catholics had to go to confession and receive communion at least once a year. Bishops were obligated to hold provincial councils. The reform of the clergy was urged. All religious communities—including new ones—had to accept the rule of either Saint Augustine or Saint Benedict in order to "reform" the new groups of religious men and women. For the 1200s, the Fourth Council of the Lateran was the main event in the history of the Western Church.

The establishment of the "new orders" has to be seen as a continuation of the reform movement begun in 1000. These new orders were many, but those that remain better known to us are the Dominicans, the Franciscans, the Servites, and the Mercedarians. All began as reform groups and continue as such within the Roman Catholic Church today.

The outstanding people in this century were certainly Francis of Assisi (1181-1226) and Clare of Assisi (1193-1253). The Franciscan movement these two laypeople established has become one of the most powerful spiritual movements the Roman Catholic Church has ever experienced. Even today, Francis in particular is well known and admired. Not only Catholics, but Protestants and members of many other major religions hold Francis of Assisi in high regard. In the entire millennium, 1000 to 2000, a layman, Francis of Assisi, remains among the top ten leaders of the Roman Catholic Church.

Pope Innocent III is one of the major leaders of this century because of the impact of the Fourth Lateran Council.

Saint Thomas Aquinas (1225-1274) also ranks among the most influential Roman Catholics of this century. He was a major leader in theology, and his influence remains powerful in the western Church. Often when people refer to "Catholic theology" today, they are talking about the theology of Thomas Aquinas. Since Augustine, no other individual has had as much theological influence as Thomas.

1300

MAIN EVENT	MAIN LEADERS
Crusades	Saint Catherine of Siena
Great Schism (1378-1417),	(1347-1380)
during which there were	Giotto di Bondone,
three popes at the same time	Florentine master painter
	Dante Alighieri, Italy's greatest
	poet (1254-1321)

For laypeople, this century did not begin well. Pope Boniface VIII, in his bull of 1296, began with this idea: "Antiquity teaches us, and the experience of the present time makes clear, that the laity are hostile to the clergy; inasmuch as not content with their own bounds, they aim at what is forbidden them. ... Nor do they reflect that power over ecclesiastical persons and goods which has been denied them." Boniface VIII was writing against the French king, Philip the Fair, who had taxed the clergy. Boniface was demanding an absolute plenitude of power for the pope, which meant that even lay leaders, even a king or emperor, was "under" the pope. The effect of Boniface's pope-first position lasted into the nineteenth century, when the pope was declared infallible. It has been present in the twentieth and twenty-first centuries, given that the pope's power over Catholic life seemed to include a Catholic political leader and his stance on moral issues (John Kennedy and the political discussion in 2004).

In the first part of the century, the crusades were the major events even though the last two crusades, the fourth (1202-1204) and fifth (1217-1221), ended in failure. The Arabs dominated the Holy Land, and the Eastern churches were under severe pressure. In the last part of the century, the papacy fell into disgrace with the emergence of three popes, all of whom had some degree of a rightful claim and some degree of an illegitimate claim to be pope. Each had what we call today a *titulus coloratus,* a spotty title. The major reason the Great Schism ended was the reform effort of the Holy Roman Emperor, a layperson, Sigismund. Without his leadership and intervention, there would never have been a Council of Constance (1414-1418), at which the papal schism was ended.

One of the main leaders of this century was Saint Catherine of Siena (1347-1380). This laywoman was a mystic and writer who is now a doctor of the Church. Catherine began a spiritual movement, and her disciples included several priests. The Dominicans took her and her cause under their protection. Catherine acted as a mediator between ecclesial and civil authorities. She was a key leader who brought about the return of one of the three popes from Avignon to Rome. Her leadership as a woman certainly indicates a tremendous development in the involvement of laity in Church leadership. Giotto di Bondone and Dante Alighieri became celebrated Catholic lay leaders. Through painting and poetry, these two men influenced thousands of people, and their influence continues today, showing that Church leadership takes place not only through the official channels of the hierarchy or the magisterium, but through the channels of literature, art, music, and drama as well. Each century has its own set of artistic leaders, and the fourteenth century was especially honored by these two men.

1400

MAIN EVENT	MAIN LEADERS
End of papal schism	Emperor Sigismund,
Fall of Constantinople	who ended the papal schism
Beginning of the renaissance	Ferdinand and Isabella, King and
popes	Queen of Aragon-Castille
	Marsilius of Padua (12801343)

The resolution of the question of who was the correct pope brought a certain sense of peace to the Church. The lay leadership of Sigismund proved to be the only leadership able to bring an end to this papal disgrace. The union of the Spanish kingdoms Aragon and Castille under Ferdinand and Isabella set the stage for a powerful colonialization and a Catholic Christianization of the non-European world that would never have taken place without their leadership.

Marsilius of Padua became the major intellectual spokesman against the claims of Pope Boniface VIII on the plenitude of papal power. Marsilius taught that the people themselves are the source of political power, basing his position for reform on the writings of two Franciscans: Johannes Duns Scotus (1266-1308) and William of Ockham (1285-1347). In England, educated laypeople were also making demands on the structures of the Church. We find this call for reform in the writings of Oxford University theologian John Wycliffe (1330-1334). Wycliffe was a priest, but many of his followers, called Lollards, were educated laymen and laywomen who were continuing the spirit of the Magna Carta (1215). This movement for the fundamental rights of citizens is also part of the reform movement of the Church, and lay leaders such as Marsilius were very prominent. The rise of the communes throughout Italy, sparked by lay leadership, was also a major part of this reform movement.

1500

MAIN EVENT	MAIN LEADERS
Arrival of Columbus in the Western Hemisphere (1492)	Christopher Columbus and other leaders of colonization
Protestant Reformation	Ignatius of Loyola and the establishment of the Jesuits
Council of Trent	Martin Luther, John Calvin, Huldrych Zwingli
	Henry V of England
	Saint Teresa of Ávila
	Saint Thomas More

The Hapsburg House, which governed Austria-Hungary and, from 1526, the Spanish empire as well, assured a strong Catholic presence. These were lay leaders. Henry IV of France accepted Catholicism rather than Protestantism.

The arrival of Columbus in Hispaniola in 1492 began a major movement of colonization and Catholic Christianization, a movement that in many ways made Roman Catholicism a world religion rather than a European religion. On the heels of this expansion, however, a major rupture began to take place: the Protestant Reformation, an integral part of the reform movement begun around 1000. When the reform initiatives of Roman Catholics—Luther, Calvin, and Zwingli—began, there was no thought of a divided Western Church. These leaders wanted a major reform in the papacy and in the papal curia; they believed that if reform occurred at this level of Church authority, reform in theology would follow. The popes and the papal curia were seen as advocating a theology that contradicted Catholic tradition and even part of the Bible. The Protestant reform must be seen at first as a "Catholic reform"; in ways similar to the reforms that occurred from 1000 to 1500, pressure was put on the highest leadership of the Church. However, since even the continued pressure of these earlier reform movements had not brought about a change in the papacy and the papal curia, the pressure finally blew open with major force. The reluctance of the pope and the curia, even in the early days of the still-Catholic Luther and Calvin, indicated that the hierarchy was not at all interested in major reform. The results of this magisterial ineptitude were catastrophic.

It took much pressure from Catholic political lay leaders in the middle of the sixteenth century to get Pope Paul III to convene the Council at Trent (1545). The first group of bishops at Trent for its inauguration and convocation numbered ten, an insignificant fraction of the entire hierarchy. Trent started on very wobbly feet because of the political machinations of both the pope and the political leaders. When the council concluded in 1563 after many fits and starts, it had accomplished much by way of doctrine and reform. The effect of Trent has remained part of Roman Catholic life to this day.

Political leaders—that is, emperors and kings—as well as clerical leaders were key to the success of the Council of Trent. However, some well-educated lay leaders were also very important. Paul III had appointed laymen to be the main leaders of the council: Gasparo Contarini, Reginald Pole, Marcello Cervini, and Ludovico Nogarola. Laymen presiding over a major council of the Church! Lay leadership had certainly moved far from where it was in 1000.

1600

MAIN EVENT	MAIN LEADERS
Counter-reform	Saint Robert Bellarmine, main
Jansenism	leader of the counter-reform
	Cornelius Jansen (1585-1638)

In the century following the Protestant Reformation and the Council of Trent, the Roman Catholic Church became very defensive and apologetic. The "tone" this gave to the theology of Church slowly took over from 1600 to the French Revolution. Robert Bellarmine was one of the main leaders of the counter-reform. His theology of Church, which stressed the Church's institutional and hierarchical aspects and its validity over all other churches (the defensive and apologetic approach), influenced the general understanding of Church for the next few centuries.

Cornelius Jansen wrote a book, *Augustinus,* which was published after his death. Jansen was a major scholar on Augustine's works and knew the writings of Augustine very well. The Abbé de Saint-Cyran published *Augustinus* and with the help of the Arnauld family started a movement, Jansenism, that required confession prior to receiving the Eucharist. The movement involved a spirituality that was basically sin oriented and prevented many people from receiving the Eucharist. The Jansenists tended to see themselves as the true Church within the wider, less-holy Church. The effects of

Jansenism are still present in parts of the western world today. The political fighting between Jesuits and Jansenists did not help the development of a solid theology of Church based on the gospels.

The defensive stance of the Church against Protestantism also created a Church leadership that was clerical and defensive against encroachment by the laity. Lay leadership was looked upon as part of Protestantism. Thus, the counter-reform of the Catholic Church included an anti-lay bias.

Galileo and Newton took up ideas from Copernicus, and a struggle between Church leadership and science began. The defense by Church leadership against the development of the natural sciences pitted educated laypeople against the hierarchy.

1700

MAIN EVENT	MAIN LEADERS
French and American Revolutions	Christian Brothers: largest group of religious brothers, founded 1680, expanded in 1700s

Both the French and American Revolutions affected the Catholic Church in a severe way. The French Revolution was decidedly anti-Catholic. At that time, all bishops in France belonged to the aristocracy and voted for the king. Only some priests belonged to the lower house. The ideas of "Fraternité, Egalité, Liberté" and "all men [and women] are created equal" were against a hierarchical way of thinking. The Catholic Church at the end of the 1700s became very defensive and reactionary. Leadership remained hierarchical and clerical.

1800

MAIN EVENTS	MAIN LEADERS
Vast emigration of Catholics from Europe to United States	Saint Elizabeth Ann Bayley Seton
	Catholics and labor unions
Rise of Marxism	Marc Sangnier and *Le Sillon*
	Rose Hawthorne Lathrop

The emigration of many Catholics from Europe to the United States and to South and Central America produced a hierarchical-control reaction by the bishops of the United States. Immigrants were to stay in the major cities and remain under hierarchical surveillance. However, Catholic laymen and laywomen began speaking out. Catholic lay congresses took place in the United States and in Europe, bringing up issues of feminism, racism, intellectual freedom, and lay leadership. With Pope Pius IX, yet another anti-lay movement took over, and all Catholic lay movements were either restricted or rejected (congresses, *Le Sillon*). The relationship between Church and state became a major issue. Are the "people" the basic source of "government"? Inalienable human rights became a major issue. Tolerance versus antagonism towards Protestants and members of non-Christian religions began to surface. Social ills became a major issue. Leo XIII's encyclical, *Rerum Novarum,* is seen as a milestone in the Church's response to social ills; it can also be seen as a paternalistic approach. A rethinking of biblical material from a historical point of view had begun in Protestantism at the end of the eighteenth century; Catholic scholars who accepted such biblical thinking were silenced and excommunicated, especially by Pius IX. Marxism was condemned outright. Catholic Marxists were persecuted.

The basis for the issues treated at Vatican II can be found in the nineteenth century. These issues already existed and were fostered by Catholic leaders, lay and, to some degree, religious and clerical: Vatican I and the issue of infallibility. The sudden end of the first

Vatican council, because Garibaldi took over Rome and all of the papal states and the Vatican no longer had a "country."

1900

MAIN EVENT	MAIN LEADERS
Two world wars and	Dorothy Day
other wars	Jean Vanier
Communism	Young Christian Workers
Major ethical issues due to	(Jocists)
science	Cesar Chavez
Vatican II	Martin Luther King, Jr.

The twentieth century was a century of wars; this affected the leadership of the Catholic Church. Many more Catholic lay leaders spoke out and demanded to be heard on issues regarding peace, sexuality, equality of women, racism, economic justice worldwide, ecumenism, and dialogue with non-Christian religions. Until Vatican II, the position of Church leadership was very defensive, apologetic, anti-lay, and punitive.

The issues taken up in Vatican II preceded the council and were voiced by laypeople and academics, both lay and cleric. Reform was a "testy" word, so "renew" became the correct word. The encyclical on birth control, *Humanae Vitae*, caused the most significant rejection of clerical authority in ethical matters. The sexual abuse by clerics and the nonethical response of bishops to this abuse caused the second most significant rejection of clerical authority in ethical matters. The moral authority of today's bishops in the United States has been radically compromised, and it will take several generations for them to regain it. Sexual abuse by clergy will remain a negative part of the entire clerical world in the United States for the next twenty to thirty years.

The Roman Catholic Church in the United States (and in the

world) needs a radical restructuring of its dominant, operative theology of Church. Until such restructuring is done, the leadership of
the Catholic Church will have only minor acceptance. The answer
to today's problems is not a return to normal. Many bishops want
their dioceses to "return to the way it was," but this spells disaster,
since the "way it was" caused today's crises. Strong and respected lay
voices will continue to criticize the hierarchical leadership of the
Church in the United States, and the men and women who voice
their concerns will become more and more a part of the leadership
of the Catholic Church in the twenty-first century.

4. Mission and Ministry

Dr. Richard Gaillardetz, University of Toledo

Late in his life, the great nineteenth-century English Catholic theologian, John Henry Newman, was supposedly asked why he had visited Rome so seldom in his long and distinguished career. Newman responded that he always found it best to heed the advice of his father, who once told him, "queasy travelers ought not visit the engine room!"

For many of us, recent events in our Church have offered an unsettling view of the ecclesiastical engine room. The crisis that has recently wracked the Church is not, in the end, a crisis occasioned by clerical sexual abuse, though instances of clerical sexual abuse indirectly instigated the crisis. No, the real crisis is not so much moral as ecclesiological. What we have discovered is that, in spite of all of the pro-Vatican II rhetoric, significant segments of our Church still operate out of an ecclesial vision uninformed by the vision of the council. We have seen the soft underbelly of our Church's decision-making processes, and it hasn't been pretty.

Crises are always unsettling for those who are affected by them, but it is worth remembering that, as Catholics, we are at home in crisis. As Father Timothy Radcliffe, former master general of the Dominican order recently remarked, Catholics' crises "are our *specialité de la maison.*"[1] One way of reading the history of our Church is to see it moving from one crisis to the next. Indeed, as Father Radcliffe observed, crises often provide the occasions for Church reform and renewal. So how must our Church respond to this crisis?

---

1. Timothy Radcliffe, "Priests and the Crisis of Hope Within the Church," *Origins* 34 (May 27, 2004):23.

I suggest that returning to the teaching of Vatican II is a good place to start. This does not mean that Vatican II has all the answers we need for moving beyond this crisis. Our Church certainly needs to work harder to fulfill the still-bracing vision of the council, but there are limits to this kind of project. It is important to recognize that in some ways we have already gone beyond the council. Our Church today is facing new challenges and questions that the council bishops never really anticipated.

One of these new challenges is the totally unanticipated flourishing of lay ministries in the four decades since the council. This development has raised important new questions about how we understand lay ministry theologically and whether preconciliar and even conciliar understandings of ordained ministry are still adequate to the situation the Church faces today. I do not think the council documents offer clear and obvious solutions for these issues, but I do think there are still resources in the conciliar teaching that can help us as we address our present situation.

When people invoke the teaching of the council on ministry in the Church, they generally turn to either *Lumen Gentium,* the Dogmatic Constitution on the Church, *Apostolicam Actuositatem,* the Decree on the Apostolate of the Lay People or *Presbyterorum Ordinis,* the Decree on the Ministry and Life of Priests. However, I would like to turn to a different document for our reflections today. The Constitution on the Sacred Liturgy, *Sacrosanctum Concilium,* was the first document to be considered by the council bishops and, though the document is explicitly concerned with the liturgy, I believe its most enduring contributions lie in what it says about the Church. Embedded in this document is the outline of a liturgical ecclesiology that might help us think about ministry in the Church today.

In article 2 of *Sacrosanctum Concilium,* the council asserted boldly that the Eucharist "is supremely effective in enabling the faithful to express in their lives and portray to others the mystery of Christ and *the real nature of the true church*" (emphasis added).

It is in the liturgy that the deepest reality of the Church is manifested. Consequently, while the Church is not Church solely when it gathers in the eucharistic synaxis, the council understood that "the liturgy is the summit *toward which* the activity of the church is directed; it is also the source *from which* all its power flows" (emphasis added, SC 10).

This suggests that a renewed vision of the Church could, and should, be read off of the corporate worship of the whole people of God.

I. Ministry Within a Liturgical Vision of the Church

In this presentation, I will draw out five features of this liturgical vision of the Church and suggest the implications for our understanding of Church ministry.

A. Rethinking Hierarchy:
The Church as an Ordered Communion

In the first chapter of the constitution, under the "The Reform of the Liturgy," we find a subsection titled "Norms Drawn From the Hierarchic and Communal Nature of the Liturgy." Though it does not appear in the text itself, this title introduces a formulation that will appear in later conciliar texts,[2] namely the assertion of the importance of being in *communio hierarchica*, "hierarchical communion," with the pope and bishops. I believe the liturgy document offers us the key to how this term might be understood. The difficulty is that by describing the Church communion as a *hierarchical*, you

---

2. LG 21, 22; *Christus Dominus* 4, 5; PO 7. It appears a sixth time in #2 of the *Nota Praevia Explicativa* attached at the 11th hour to *Lumen Gentium*, without conciliar approval, "by higher authority."

end up returning to the hierocratic, pyramidal view of the Church that developed in the thirteenth century. That view, quite foreign to the Church of the first thousand years, presented the Church as a pyramidal structure in which the fullness of power (*plenitudo potestatis*) and truth was given to the pope and shared in diminishing degrees with the lower levels of Church life.[3] One might think of this as a spiritualized, medieval precursor to "Reagonomics" or "trickledown theory." This descending chain-of-command view of hierarchy has persisted in certain sectors of the Church, in spite of the council's reforms, up to the present.

Feminist theologians have rightly challenged this pyramidal understanding of "hierarchy" as one of the many concepts used in the Church to subordinate the laity in general and women in particular. Yet perhaps the term "hierarchical" can be retained if we purge it of those pyramidal and patriarchal conceptions.[4] I contend that when the Constitution on the Sacred Liturgy refers to the "hierarchic and communal nature of the liturgy," it does not have in mind a return to a pyramidal ecclesiology. The liturgy can be said to be hierarchical, not in the sense of a chain of command or a pyramidal structure, but in the sense that the liturgy manifests the Church as an *ordered* communion with a great diversity of ministries and Christian activities that together build up the life of the Church.[5] The

---

3. See Jean Leclerq, "Influence and Noninfluence of Dionysius in the Western Middle Ages," in *Pseudo-Dionysius: The Complete Works* (New York: Paulist, 1987), 31; Yves Congar, *L'Église de Saint Augustin à l'époque moderne* (Paris: Cerf, 1970), 229-30.

4. For an attempt to retrieve the notion of "hierarchy" by distinguishing between "command hierarchy" and "participatory hierarchy," see Terence L. Nichols, *That All May Be One: Hierarchy and Participation in the Church* (Collegeville, MN: The Liturgical Press, 1997).

5. This view of the Church as an ordered communion parallels in some ways Ghislain Lafont's presentation of the postconciliar Church as a "structured communion." See his *Imagining the Catholic Church: Structured Communion in the Spirit* (Collegeville, MN: The Liturgical Press, 2000).

Church of Jesus Christ, animated by the Spirit, is now and has always been subject to Church ordering as it receives its life from the God who, in Christian faith, is ordered in eternal self-giving as a triune communion of persons.

B. The Threefold Ordering of Our Baptism

The most fundamental ordering of the Church occurs in Christian initiation. This conviction is reflected in the council's call for a fundamental reform of initiatory rites, including the restoration of the catechumenate for adults, the revision of the baptismal rite for infants, and the reconsideration of the rites of confirmation. These calls for ritual reform were in keeping with the larger agenda of the council, which is often captured in the French term, *ressourcement,* a "return to the sources." In this case, the council was reaching back to a more biblical vision of Christian initiation. Indeed, the early Church's theology of baptism might be thought of as the first Christian ecclesiology.[6]

From a biblical perspective, Christian initiation "orders" or "configures" the believer to Christ *within* the community of faith, Christ's body. Christian initiation does not just make one a different kind of individual; it draws the believer into a profound ecclesial relationship, one's ecclesial *ordo* within the life of the Church.

The distinctive character of this baptismally ordered relationship unfolds in three dimensions. Vertically, we are baptized into communion with God, in Christ, by the power of the Spirit. Yet this relationship is inseparable from our horizontal relationship with all our brothers and sisters in baptism who constitute together a communion of believers.

---

6. Gerard Austin, "Restoring Equilibrium after the Struggle with Heresy," in *Source and Summit: Commemorating Josef A. Jungmann, S.J.,* ed. Joanne M. Pierce and Michael Downey (Collegeville, MN: The Liturgical Press, 1999):37.

These two dimensions of the baptismal ordering must, in turn, be conjoined to a third dimension, the movement outward toward the world in mission. This three-dimensional ecclesial relationship established by Christian initiation offers us our primal identity as Christian believers, and it can never be abandoned. It constitutes the very essence of Christian discipleship.

Sacrosanctum Concilium reminded us, not only in its call for the reform of the rites of initiation but in its focus on the whole worshiping assembly, that our primary identity as Christians is not as lays or clerics, but as members of the baptized called to participate in the life and worship of the Church. Article 14 of the constitution speaks of full participation of the baptized in the liturgy as both a right *and an obligation.* Baptism is an ecclesial event that lays claim on our identity as Christians and demands much of us. Perhaps in all of our discussion of the rights of the baptized, we have not said enough about the real communal obligations our baptism places on us.

One of the biggest mistakes often made in interpreting the teaching of the council is the tendency to focus on the council's theology of the laity and the failure to place the council's view of the laity in the framework of its understanding of baptism. In reading the council documents closely, however, one discovers that the heart of the council's efforts to articulate a positive theology of the laity is a focus on our common baptism, a baptism that configures all believers, including the ordained, as disciples of Christ.[7] This was the import of the well-known decision to move the chapter on the people of God in front of the chapter on the hierarchy in *Lumen Gentium.* It was a symbolic expression of a profound ecclesiological principle: we must begin with what unites us (faith and baptism) before we

---

7. See Richard R. Gaillardetz, "Shifting Meanings in the Lay-Clergy Distinction." *Irish Theological Quarterly* 64 (1999):115-39.

can consider what distinguishes us (ordination). This does not deny, of course, that Christians may be further "ordered" in service of the Church by sacramental ordination. It does mean, as Bishop Franjo Šeper of Zagreb noted at the council, that the ordained do not cease being people of God after ordination; the obligations that are theirs by virtue of baptism and confirmation still remain.[8] St. Augustine knew this when he said

> *When I am frightened by what I am for you, then I am consoled by what I am with you. For you I am the bishop, with you I am a Christian. The first is an office, the second a grace; the first a danger, the second salvation.*[9]

Similar convictions regarding the priority of baptism led the late Cardinal Leon Suenens to remark that "a pope's finest moment is not that of his election or consecration, but that of his baptism."[10]

An adequate liturgical ecclesiology begins with initiation into the community of faith that gathers on the day of the resurrection to celebrate the Eucharist. The whole community of the baptized, Christ's body, is the subject of the eucharistic celebration. We remind ourselves of our baptism when we dip our hands into the baptismal waters and sign ourselves upon taking our place in the eucharistic assembly. If the liturgy is a ritual enactment of what the Church truly is, then we can say that all God's people are subjects in the life of the Church and not merely passive recipients of clerical directives. All of the baptized must share in the corporate discernment of God's will undertaken in collabo-

8. *Acta Synodalia* II/3, 202.

9. St. Augustine of Hippo, *Sermon*, 340, 1.

10. Quoted in Paul Lakeland, *The Liberation of the Laity* (New York: Continuum, 2003), 105.

ration with and under the leadership of the bishops of the Church. This right and obligation to participation in Church life does not mean lay usurpation of episcopal responsibilities, but rather an appropriation of the baptized's legitimate concern for the welfare of the Church.

This cannot be said strongly enough. The consultation and collaboration of all God's people is not an abdication of episcopal leadership, but rather a condition for its responsible and faithful exercise. To further establish this point, I would like to turn to a second feature of the liturgy document's ordering of the Church: the ministry of the bishop.

C. The Liturgical Ministry of the Ordained

If baptism constitutes the most fundamental ordering of the people of God, in the Catholic Church we believe that some among the baptized are further ordered or reconfigured for leadership in the sacrament of holy orders. And, according to the council, the fullness of orders is conferred on the bishop.

One of the most overlooked contributions of the liturgy constitution is its placement of the bishop at the center of the liturgical life of the diocese. The council asserted, moreover, that the most profound manifestation of the local Church was encountered at diocesan liturgies presided over by the bishop (LG 41).

Regrettably, the council did not explore the full implications of defining the ministry of the bishop in terms of his eucharistic presidency. In the liturgy, the bishop is placed in a relationship of reciprocity with the gathered assembly.[11] As presider, the bishop gathers

---

11. For a development of this liturgical view of the bishop, see the Joint International Commission for Theological Dialogue between the Orthodox Church and the Roman Catholic Church's document, "The Mystery of the Church and of the Eucharist in the Light of the Mystery of the Holy Trinity," in *The Quest for Unity: Orthodox and Catholics in Dialogue* (Washington, DC: United States Catholic Conference, 1996), 59.

the people of God for corporate worship, proclaims the Scriptures, receives the gifts of bread and wine from the people, offers them up to God for and with the people, and returns the gifts to the people, now transformed into the Bread of Life and Cup of Salvation. At no point in the liturgy does the Eucharist ever become the bishop's own private work; even as he engages in his unique presidential ministry, he remains in vital communion with his people.

Moreover, in the bishop's eucharistic presidency, the mutual exchange of gifts includes more than bread and wine: The very faith of the Church is offered by the people to the bishop and, as articulated in the ongoing tradition of the Church, that faith is returned to the people in the bishop's teaching and preaching. This new gift exchange reminds us that the faith the bishop is ordained to safeguard is nothing other than the faith he has received from the people. The reciprocal relationship between bishop and people enacted in the liturgy opens up an understanding of not only the bishop's sacramental ministry, but of his ministries of teaching and governance as well. It presents the bishop not as a dispenser of truth and grace, but as the one who offers to God the faith and life of those he serves as well as the eucharistic elements. The ministry of the bishop cannot be understood in isolation; it is only fully apprehended in the context of the Church at prayer.

According to Vatican II, the priest shares and collaborates in the bishop's ministry of apostolic oversight, or *episkope.* This is why the presbyter presides over any Eucharist in which the bishop is not present. The council chose not to define the bishop in terms of the priest, as had been the custom for much of the second millennium; rather, the council defined the ministry of the presbyter in terms of the bishop. The presbyter collaborates and extends the ministry of apostolic oversight entrusted to the bishop. Consequently, I would argue that the fullest theology of the presbyterate is also developed in terms of the presbyter's eucharistic presidency. In the Eucharist, the presbyter's role as liturgical president is a ritual enactment of his pastoral ministry of apostolic oversight.[12]

I would also make the case, although it cannot be developed here, that the ministry of the deacon as well must be defined in terms of the ministry of the bishop. I would argue that a careful reading of the diaconate in the early Church suggests that what defined the deacon was not what he represented as public icon, nor a particular set of ministries or tasks, but rather his close alignment with the bishop as one who served, but did not himself exercise, the bishop's ministry of apostolic oversight.

D. A Diversity of Ministries

Let us turn now to another teaching of the constitution on the liturgy. In a passage that now seems tame and obvious, the council wrote that "servers, readers, commentators, and members of the choir also *exercise a genuine liturgical ministry*" (emphasis added, SC 29). This passage would not even merit comment were it not for a consistent trend in recent Vatican pronouncements to obsess over the distinctiveness of the sacred ministry of the ordained. I have in mind not only the revised *General Instruction of the Roman Missal* and its preoccupation with the predicate *sacred,* nor the recent document on liturgical abuses, *Redemptionis Sacramentum,* but also the 1997 interdicasterial document, "Certain Questions Regarding Collaboration of the Lay Faithful in Ministry of Priests."[13] The sense one

---

12. I realize that this raises questions regarding priests who are professed religious and for diocesan priests who are not engaged in parish ministry. This is a complicated issue that cannot be fully addressed here. Let me simply say that I think these developments in the theology of the priesthood emerged as historical accommodations to pressing pastoral needs and therefore constitute legitimate exceptions. But, generally speaking, one theologizes from the norm rather than from the exception.

13. "Some Questions Regarding Collaboration of Nonordained Faithful in Priests' Sacred Ministry," *Origins 27* (November 27, 1997):397-410.

gets in documents such as these is that the only way to enhance the dignity of the ordained is to build an ontologic wall between the ordained and all other ministers of the Church.

How far removed this seems from the intention of the council fathers! What the constitution says of liturgical ministries is true for all ministries in the Church. There is no competition in the life of public service on behalf of the Church. Lectors, eucharistic ministers, ministers of hospitality, deacons, priests, and bishops—these ministries do not compete with one another in the liturgy, but cooperate in a wonderful way to build up the body of Christ at worship.

This sense of liturgical cooperation must extend as well to our understanding of all ecclesial ministries. What distinguishes the bishop from the priest from the deacon from the lector is not, as it used to be thought, the question of power. A liturgical ecclesiology does not begin with a delineation of which unique powers the bishop has that the priest doesn't or of what power the priest has that the deacon doesn't. Rather, liturgical ecclesiology begins with the unique ministerial relationship of the bishop; the bishop's role cannot be filled by the deacon or lector, but that does not make the bishop intrinsically superior to the deacon or lector. The liturgy establishes ministries according to a diversity of ministerial relations, not according to a descending hierarchy of ministerial powers. Anyone familiar with the conduct of relationships within a typical diocesan chancery or parish pastoral team can assure you that we are far from realizing the respectful mutuality of ministerial relationships enacted in each liturgical celebration.

E. Liturgy of the Church, Liturgy of the World

The final and perhaps most important reason for situating a theology of ministry within the liturgy is that the celebration of the liturgy is always in view of the Church's mission in the world. As Christians, we are baptized into mission. This mission is no mere extrinsic task imposed upon the Church from without; it is the very *raison d'être* of the Church. Indeed, the Church's mission derives from its Trinitarian origins. Salvation history reveals a God who sends forth the word and Spirit in mission as the very expression and fulfillment of God's love for the world. God's word, spoken into human history from the beginning of creation and made effective by the power of the Spirit, in the fullness of time became incarnate as Jesus of Nazareth.

The origins of the Church, in turn, are inextricably linked to Jesus' gathering of a community of followers who, after his death and resurrection, were empowered by his Spirit to continue his mission to serve, proclaim, and realize the coming reign of God. The Pastoral Constitution on the Church in the Modern World states that the whole Church which "is to be a leaven and, as it were, the soul of human society in its renewal by Christ and transformation into the family of God" (GS 40). Later in that same article, the council members spoke of the mission of the Church to heal and elevate the dignity of the human person, to strengthen human society, and to help humanity discover the deeper meaning of daily life. "The Church, then, believes that *through each of its members and its community as a whole* it can help to make the human family and its history still more human" (emphasis added, GS 40).

This firm orientation of the baptized as being bound together in a common mission is a most necessary foundation for any consideration of Church ministry. It serves as a vital correction against any tendency to allow practical distinctions between the Church *ad intra* and the Church *ad extra* to turn into a dichotomizing separation. All Church ministry is fundamentally oriented toward the Church's mission to the world in the service of God's reign.

Only from a liturgical framework that sees the entire community of the baptized entering, in ritual and in symbol, into the dynamism of the trinitarian missions of word and Spirit, sending forth the entire people of God in service of God's reign, can we properly grasp the missionary orientation of *all* Church ministry. This sending forth from the eucharistic liturgy to undertake the liturgy of the world sees *all* ministry, ordained and nonordained, as oriented toward the coming reign of God. As the late Father Robert Hovda was so fond of saying, in every liturgy we "play the kingdom." It is in the liturgy that we "act out the reign of God, the reign of justice and peace, for it is toward that end that we must move ourselves and our world."[14] We enact, if only for an hour, a world transformed by God's shalom. When the baptized gather at the eucharistic synaxis, it is to celebrate this Christian vocation to mission.

The great orthodox theologian Alexander Schmemann wrote that the liturgy "is not an escape from the world, rather it is the arrival at a vantage point from which we can see more deeply into the reality of the world."[15] Consequently, as another orthodox theologian put it, we are sent forth from the Eucharist to celebrate "the liturgy after the liturgy."[16] Karl Rahner had much the same thing in mind when he wrote of the "liturgy of the world."[17] What we celebrate in word and sacrament effects the transformation of our eucharistic gifts and the community itself. The liturgical transformation impels us into the world in which we serve the reign of God in the world's ongoing transformation.

---

14. Robert Hovda, *The Amen Corner,* ed. John F. Baldovin (Collegeville, MN: The Liturgical Press, 1994), 19-20.

15. Alexander Schmemann, *For the Life of the World* (Crestwood, NY: St. Vladimir's Press, 1973), 27.

16. Ion Bria, *The Liturgy after the Liturgy* (Geneva: World Council of Churches, 1996).

17. Karl Rahner, "On the Theology of Worship," in *Theological Investigations,* vol. 19 (New York: Crossroads, 1983), 141-49; idem, "Considerations on the Active Role of the Person in the Sacramental Event," in *Theological Investigations,* vol. 14 (New York: Seabury, 1976), 161-84. See also Michael Skelley, *The Liturgy of the World: Karl Rahner's Theology of Worship* (Collegeville, MN: Liturgical Press, 1991).

II. Some Modest Proposals for the Church

In the light of this liturgical framing of the question of ministry in the Church, I make two concrete proposals for Church reform:

A. Reconfiguration of the discernment and formation processes associated with ordination to the presbyterate and episcopate

Vatican II's Constitution on the Sacred Liturgy made an important ecclesiological contribution when it grounded the ministry of the bishop in his liturgical presidency of the Church at worship. This liturgical foundation reminds us that the bishop and the presbyters who share in his ministry, engage preeminently in the ministry of *episkope*, or pastoral oversight, which takes its ritual form in the presidency at the Eucharist.

This pastoral oversight represents but one form of leadership within the Church, and it is the only form that ordinarily must be exercised by a bishop or presbyter. I believe it is crucial that our Church begin reconfiguring vocational discernment and seminary formation programs in view of this emphasis on the presbyter as a pastoral leader responsible for apostolic oversight of a eucharistic community. Such a vision would demand a dramatic shift in the qualities the Church looks for in its candidates for presbyteral ministry. It would mean seeking out candidates for presbyteral ordination who demonstrate the ability to recognize, discern, and empower the many charisms of the baptized community.

We should not underestimate the significance of this shift. During ten years of seminary teaching I have observed that, in our current ecclesiastical context, those who engage in vocations work and those responsible for seminary formation often find themselves, against their own instincts, looking for a clear impediment to priestly ministry instead of a charism for pastoral leadership. What we see, in other words, is not the positive discernment of charisms, but the negative discernment of impediments.

Let me put the matter bluntly. If a particular seminarian shows up regularly for community prayer and meetings, dispatches his community responsibilities without complaint, passes his seminary courses, and does not commit some egregious moral offense, this candidate will be ordained to the priesthood even if there is no discernible evidence of a charism for pastoral leadership, preaching, teaching, or pastoral counseling.

This same commitment to linking episcopal and presbyteral ministry to the ministry of *episkope*, or apostolic oversight, has clear implications for the process by which bishops are selected. In a recent correspondence with *National Catholic Reporter* Vatican correspondent, John Allen, I proposed that the ideal resume of a candidate currently seeking an episcopal appointment would list these five qualifications: a) protégé of an influential cardinal, b) pontifical degree from a Roman university, c) tour of duty in a curial post, d) experience as a seminary teacher or rector, and e) no record of having written or said anything that might be construed as critical of official magisterial pronouncements or Church policies.

Notably absent from this list is demonstrated ability as pastoral leader. Presumably, this qualification is currently viewed as ecclesiastical gravy.

B. The development and implementation of guidelines/ standards for lay ministries that would include rituals of installation and commissioning

So-called lay ecclesial ministries have matured sufficiently to justify a standardization and formalization of such ministries, accompanied by a commensurate ritualization. An important development in this regard is the recently approved *National Certification Standards for Lay Ecclesial Ministers* produced collaboratively by the National Association for Lay Ministry, the National Federation for Catholic Youth Ministry, and the National Conference for

Catechetical Leadership in conjunction with the United States Conference of Catholic Bishops commission on certification and accreditation. The result of this process was a set of certification standards applicable for four lay ministries: 1) pastoral associate, 2) parish-life coordinator, 3) parish catechetical leader, and 4) youth-ministry leader.

When Pope Paul VI suppressed minor orders and created the installed ministries of lector and acolyte, he invited bishops' conferences to propose other significant stable ministries that might become installed ministries requiring extended formation and, presumably, a formal ritual of installation. I believe the time is ripe to create formal, installed ministries along the lines of the four ministries mentioned earlier. Movement in this direction would encourage a view of lay ministries as significant public ministries in service of the Church defined by the ritual installation by which they are called into service rather than by the designation *lay*, which too often defines the minister by what he or she is not, namely, ordained.

Beyond ministries that demand significant ministerial formation and a high degree of stability (ordained and installed ministries), there are still other ordered ministries, the undertaking of which does still place one in a new ecclesial relationship. These might include parish catechists, liturgical ministers who proclaim God's word (lectors), lead the community in sung prayer (cantors), distributors of Communion at the eucharistic assembly and to those absent due to infirmity (extraordinary ministers of Communion), and providers of liturgical hospitality and order (ushers and greeters). These ministries imply a new degree of accountability, a specialized formation, and a demand for some formal authorization that distinguishes them from the exercise of other baptismal charisms evident, for example, in parenting or daily Christian witness. At the same time, these ministries will generally be governed at a more local level. The determination of the specific requirements for formation and the particular form the ritualization of their ministry takes (liturgical commissioning) will generally occur at the level of the parish or the diocese.

I believe this proposal, though institutional in its orientation, would go a long way toward moving our vision of ministry from our current preoccupation with the lay versus ordained question to a vision of a Church built up by the many charisms of the whole people of God and by the many ordered ministries of the Church, some of which are ordered through sacramental ordination, others by installation, and still others by diocesan or parish commission.

These proposals are by no means cure-alls. But they do orient us toward the need to make incremental, pragmatic steps in Church structures that can help reinforce an emerging theology of ministry adequate to the new ministerial reality our Church faces today. Without such concrete steps, our Church risks squandering an enormous opportunity to take advantage of the passion of so many eager to serve the Church. We do not suffer from a shortage of laborers for the harvest; what we suffer from is a lack of vision regarding how to best honor their gifts and how to most effectively make use of these many laborers in service of the Church and its mission.

5. Lay Ecclesial Ministry— What It Is and What It Isn't

Rev. Thomas F. O'Meara, O.P., University of Notre Dame

Stimulated by Vatican II, the Roman Catholic Church has expanded its field of ministries over the past thirty-five years. In the years following the council, ministry changed rapidly. The local church changed by dramatically increasing the number of people at work in parishes and dioceses and by setting up parish ministries of education, liturgy, or social justice. And the very model of parish changed: from priests in the sanctuary and sisters in the school to a staff of full-time ministers in a parish community led by the pastor, each with his or her education, expertise, natural gifts, charisms, and commissions.[1] The division between priests and active religious and a passive laity, or the frustrated attempt to create some kind of separate apostolate for the laity in the world but without any activity in the Church—these faded.

This newness in ministry was, in fact, something old: a renewal of biblical community, a restoration of aspects of the reality to which New Testament ecclesiology witnessed. The new parish life of ministry was founded on theologies of baptism, theologies unfolded by European theologians after World War II. For instance, in 1953 the journal of the important institute for religious education in Brussels, *Lumen Vitae*—which introduced the entire world to the field of religious education—had a special issue on the Holy Ghost in the Church and in baptism. The next year (1954), a special issue on the sacraments contained essays like "The Action of the Holy Ghost in Baptism" and "The Bible and Baptism."

---

1. Winfried Haunerland, "The Heirs of the Clergy? The New Pastoral Ministries and the Reform of the Minor Orders," *Worship* 75 (2001), 305-320.

The following pages reflect on baptism and ministry and initiation into Christian life and ministry. This theme may still hold some seminal insights. In one of the last interviews he gave, Yves Congar observed of the postconciliar time, "There are certainly many new things. What I wrote in 1935 concerning the laity is of course long outdated. The laity have been led to take on many roles in the Church. Laypeople have become more conscious of the reality of baptism, a baptism which makes them active members of the Mystical Body of Christ."[2]

Part I: The *Pneuma*

The man or woman entering the community of the Church by baptism receives the Spirit of the risen Christ. These words express a reality that is most basic in Christianity. The Spirit, the *Pneuma,* of the risen Jesus, the Holy Spirit, is presented in Saint Paul's letters as a source of a life that includes ministry. Could the divine Spirit touch our spirit? Christian faith says yes. The first Christians knew they were not worshiping God at a distance or God enclosed in a sacred precinct, in a temple. God comes intimately into the life of each human being: the Spirit is in us. The eighth chapter of Paul's Letter to the Romans presents this theology. "For the law of the Spirit of life in Christ Jesus has set you free…" (8:2). Certainly Paul is speaking paradoxically, for "law" here is not a new set of rules but a realm of reality. Joseph Fitzmyer comments, "In union with Christ, then, Christians come under the 'law' of the Spirit that gives life. Thus qualified, *nomos* no longer refers to the Mosaic law. Paul indulges in oxymoron as he now applies *nomos* to the Spirit, which in his understanding is anything but 'law.' Rather, the law of the Spirit is nothing other than the 'Spirit of God' (8:9a, 14) or the 'Spirit of Christ'

---

2. Congar in Frano Prcela, "Pionier der kirchlichen Erneuerung," *Wort und Wahrheit* 36 (1995), 133.

(8:9b)....It is the dynamic 'principle' of the new life, creating vitality and separating humans from sin and death....It is the life-giving Spirit of God himself, which 'dwells' in the justified Christian (8:9)."[3] Paul describes enthusiastically "those who live according to the Spirit" (8:5); the baptized "are in the Spirit" (8:9). Paul reaches a climax: "...the Spirit of God dwells in you" (8:9). Fitzmyer concludes, "Christ dwells in Christians as his Spirit becomes the source of the new experience, empowering them in a new way and with a new vitality."[4] Liturgical historian Aidan Kavanaugh wrote of baptismal life: "It must be remembered that the baptism of Christians was not Johannine but Christic; it was a baptism not of water but of the Holy Spirit. The water bath is a function of the Spirit."[5]

Romans also refers to the power of the Holy Spirit working for the expansion of the Church (15:15, 16). In later chapters, not the word *Pneuma*, but *Xapis*, "grace," grace in facets of grace called "charisms," flows into and sustains ministry. The community, although "one body in Christ" (12:5), has "gifts that differ according to the grace given to us..." (12:6), and Paul mentions specific ministries: discernment in things of religion, preaching, ministry or being a deacon, and teachers.

The Spirit's life in us is not primarily an insurance policy for heaven, not a baseball card of Church membership, and not a plug that connects us to an electric company of actual graces. God is present in us according to the mode of a life. This is not surprising; after all, we are living creatures, creatures living through intelligence and freedom and religious aspirations at a high level. Life manifests

---

3. Fitzmyer, *Romans: A New Translation with Introduction and Commentary* (New York: Doubleday, 1992), 482-83.

4. Ibid., 290. "Through faith and baptism justified Christians are not only 'in the Spirit,' but the Spirit is now said to dwell in them."

5. Aidan Kavanaugh, *The Shape of Baptism: The Rite of Christian Initiation* (New York: Pueblo Publishing, 1978), 25.

itself in activities. If the Spirit's life is a life, it will be a source of activity. Life is the opposite of sleep or coma or death, and a religious life will be the opposite of being religiously passive, fearful, marginal, or demeaned. God is active, and every living being is active. The kingdom of God is not a haven, not a holy place apart, but a milieu where the Spirit brings not laws and rituals, but a life. Faith's ideas express the acceptance of a new life.

What is surprising is that early Christians presume that such a life overflows essentially into activity. Grace leads to charisms and charisms to ministry; ministry is actions serving within the Church and around the Church. They build up the Church.[6] Being a new kind of human being as the image of God from creation, existing in Jesus Christ, being touched by the Spirit—these do not end in a theology of a Christian woman or man being a work of art or being an icon in the corner of a monastic garden (although those images can inspire our private meditations); they end in life and activity.

Part II: Life in the Church

The Spirit of God is a principle of human life. The view of the Church in the first centuries presumed that Christian existence, at times in our lives, leads into ministry.

Every ministry begins with the Spirit and presumes baptismal life. Every Christian receives potentially—or really, over a lifetime—a calling to some ministry. Speaking about one's faith, evangelizing others, being a parent, and serving others is life from the Spirit. This is, too, the theology of the image of the Body of Christ. Jürgen Roloff wrote, "The ideal Pauline community is perhaps best described as a

---

6. The Jerusalem biblical scholar M. E. Boismard wrote in 1956 in *Lumière et Vie* of the newness of baptism. For an adult it is something of a "rupture" because it is a "new creation" of the baptized. The Christian is a new kind of human with her activities, a new kind of image of God (who is activity). See M. E. Boismard, "Baptême et Renouveau," *Lumière et Vie*, 27 (1956), 405.

pneumatocractic community of service.[7] This includes acknowledging the ultimate power in the Church to be with the Spirit. The Church is community and service, not monarchy or democracy, but an organization that through the Spirit furthers life and ministry, a community of graced rights and activities and voices of the faithful.

Part III: Counterforces

To repress life's activities is dangerous. When human life is repressed, suppressed, the person becomes sick, becomes neurotic, becomes moribund. What happens when life in the Spirit is repressed? Church leadership and pastoral theologians and religious psychologists could explore this question more. Repression of human life causes anger and frustration. If the angry person is free, socially free, theologically free, he or she may well leave the Church. The fourth largest religious group in America is nonpracticing Catholics. (Growing up in Des Moines, Iowa, I was not precocious but, by the time I was ten, I knew that friends of my parents who did not go to Church did not do so because they had problems with the theory of Trinitarian perichoresis, but with the Sunday Mass and the pastor.)

Some may view the angry as disobedient or heterodox and may view those departing as apostates. Still, healthy people reject the repression of their spiritual life. Nonpractice has nothing to do with eating McDonald's® hamburgers too often (the new pastoral theology of the Vatican), but with ignoring and silencing the baptized. A psychology of grace, an ecclesiology of the Spirit, can address the millions who believe but are not active in the Church, men and

---

7. "Human beings can be helpers of the Spirit, fulfilling the Spirit's tasks and instructions, but their action is only *subsidiary....*For Paul, Church leadership is primarily a function of the specific local assembly. His image that the life of this assembly is similar to an organism is suggestive because through it both basic ideas—*leadership by the Spirit and service*—seem to be completely realized." Jürgen Roloff, "Church Leadership According to the NT," *Theology Digest* 44:2 (Summer 1997), 139, 143.

women who may be waiting not for a canonical exception or a minimalist creed but for life in the community.

Aidan Kavanaugh wrote of developments over centuries of Church life that "occluded" baptism, that is, blocked baptism as the moon can eclipse the sun. Religious life and priesthood were "baptismal surrogates." For centuries, baptism was pushed into the background. Religious life and orders created a first-class citizenship, while the baptized were placed in a state passive and bland—they were "a proletariat." To associate baptismal reality and its attendant piety with something less than the entire Christian reality, Kavanaugh concluded, is wrong. Its purpose may be control, for to diminish baptism helps control the baptized.[8]

Among forces obscuring or diminishing the life of the Spirit in the baptized are three theologies: one of baptism, one of Church authority, and one of the priesthood. They are not false perspectives, and they were successful in their times. But like all theologies, they have a limited shelf life, are partial truths; what was once their truth can in different times be a half-truth.

1. Theology of Baptism

Its origins are medieval, but it flourished after Trent and after 1850. This perspective holds that baptism is mainly a divine action on the private soul. The baptized soul at death is recognized and admitted into heaven (or, more often, purgatory). Baptism ensures that the person no longer bears some stain that makes him or her the enemy of God. Subsequently, in the short time before their deaths, the baptized should guard against sins of sexuality, dishonesty, and heresy. This theology had little to offer in terms of public human life and

---

8. Kavanaugh, 158-160; see also Nathan Mitchell, "Dissolution of the Rite of Initiation," in *Made, Not Born. New Perspectives on Christian Initiation and the Catechumenate*, ed. John Galen (Notre Dame: University of Notre Dame Press, 1976), 5072.

life in the Church, family, or society. Christian life existed largely in the spirituality of a soul (rarely accessible to laypeople) or in the life to come after death.

2. Theology of Church Authority

The second theology views authority in the Church as a neoplatonic hierarchy, a ladder, stairs running from heaven to earth. (*Hierarchy* means a *sacral principate,* that is, an organized group ruling others in religion.) To note the theological language and format of *hierarchy* is not to challenge authority in the Church. Authority can assume different forms. One can retain the understanding of authority in bishops and the bishop of Rome but insist that the structure-and-thought form should not be a static descending hierarchy, a sacral pyramid.

This theology entered the Church six hundred years after Pentecost, in a Platonic Middle Eastern world where descending and ascending movements of truth and light in a world of darkness were prominent. It was applied to the Church because it was asserted to be basic, ruling the structure of every organization, even the world of angels.

This theology is a pyramid of Christians, with those below subject to those above. Because its movement is only downward, the beings away from the top of the pyramid have nothing to contribute upward. Those above them are brighter, more gifted, and better educated. The higher-ups are, in their very being, better in every way. There is no illumination upward; no one on the ladder can or will learn from those below them.

This hierarchical model entered the West in the form of medieval feudalism. As knights and barons served dukes and king, a chain of clerical servants reached up to the pope.[9] That model of author-

---

9. See Hans Küng, *My Struggle for Freedom* (Grand Rapids: Eerdmans, 2003), 348.

ity was not previous Church Tradition, and it is difficult to imagine Jesus approving of it.

3.   Theology of the Priesthood

The third perspective that obscures the life of the Spirit in the baptized is a view of the priesthood drawn from the important age of French spirituality in the seventeenth century.

This theology was part of a valuable renewal of the priest's spiritual life through seminary education in an effort to make him more than just the recipient of a salary for doing a job for which only a few Catholics qualify. The priest is a spiritual director, a teacher in preaching, and the source of the Eucharist. The spiritualities of "the French school"—new congregations like the Vincentians and Sulpicians and influential figures like Pierre de Bérulle and Jean Eudes—offered a theology of the priest founded upon a physical, actually a metaphysical, identity with Jesus Christ as the Incarnate Word.

The nature of this very close identification is left vague because each priest does not resemble Jesus physically or biologically. The priest was another Christ and had a sacredness in his being. Where? In his hands? In his soul? In his body? This identification of priest with Jesus of Nazareth led, in turn, to Jesus Christ as the Incarnate Word. We should note that the personal relationship soon referred to the logos as much as to Jesus. The unction with which Jesus Christ was consecrated high priest is the divinity itself. Priests are clothed with the very person of Jesus Christ. "For the priesthood is a state that is holy and sacred in its institution; it is an office that is divine in its operation and in its ministry; and it is, moreover, the origin of all the holiness which must be in the Church of God. The priesthood calls for a very particular bond with Jesus Christ, our Lord, with whom we are joined in a special manner by our priestly ministry, and through a power so elevated that even the angels in their state of glory are not worthy of it."[10]

The priest in the Church is like a living Jesus Christ who is head of the Church, who has a plenitude of grace and divine riches for his own perfection and for all people. The priest is another Christ, mainly in being. Priesthood contains all of the Church's ministry, and the priest is the only ministry. Where it is, there is the Church.

Close identification with Jesus is mediated through confecting the Eucharist, which displays the divine side of the priest through the elevation of the host after the consecration at Mass (not with Eucharistic communion). The priest's ministry is divinely effective, because it occurs automatically in prescribed rites and Latin words.

Jacques Maritain wrote in 1971 that this theology confused the sanctity to which a priest is called with a state of life bestowed by the sacrament of orders, separating the priest from the people and confusing a state of life with functions. Christ is not a priest solely or mainly by virtue of the hypostatic union but by the actions his graced human nature pursues. A man does not become a conjoined physical instrument of a divine person by being ordained. Maritain spoke of an ill-conceived process of "transpersonalization" occurring during ordination, leading the priest to an "illusory sublimation."[11]

Recent problems flowed from the priest being valuable apart from how well he acts in the public forum of the Church and how well he preaches or counsels or empowers the parish. To mention an exaggeration in this particular spirituality is not to diminish the importance of the spiritual life of a presbyter, bishop, deacon, or anyone in ministry.

---

10. Bérulle, *Opuscule de piété*, 192:2 (Paris: Migne, 1857), col. 1270.

11. Jacques Maritain, "Á Propos de l'École Française," *Revue Thomiste* 71 (1971) 465, 469, 471. He links a hierarchical theology with an ontology of being a priest. "I think that it is Pseudo-Denys and his hierarchies that are responsible for the obscurity that one finds in unsatisfactory formulas" (465).

Part IV: Theological Critique

Quite dominant from 1650 to 1950, these three theologies were judged by Vatican II to be theologies of an individual, not theologies of a community or the Church. They supported an eschatology of the soul, a feudalism in Church authority, and a daily supernatural event. They had their value when life was short, society feudal, and the baptized uneducated, but they are less helpful today when the Church is so large, so varied, so public. However, each challenges Jesus' preaching of how the kingdom of God relates to all men and women as a new creation and obscures Paul's theology of baptism; each diminishes the phrase of Vatican II that there is among all the baptized "a true equality" (LG 32).

This theology of baptism looks at the individual mainly in terms of the next life or of a spiritual life to which the laity has little access. It has now almost disappeared. We do not explain baptism or grace as insurance in a hostile and dark world for Christians soon to die into a better life. It is much more. The liturgical readings, Rite of Christian Initiation for Adults, baptismal sacrament, and parish life no longer present baptism in this way.

This theology of Church authority is not about most Christians at all—they are at the bottom of the pyramid, inactive. Yves Congar wrote of the ecclesiology flourishing in the years from Vatican I to Vatican II: "If authority is exercised well, then order will be assured. This order is unitary and ultimately hierocratic. The people are at the base of the pyramid."[12] Already in the thirteenth century, Thomas Aquinas had to point out the limits of this to permit pastoral changes for the Middle Ages such as friars and universities. The Church hierarchy, he wrote, does not reproduce the heavenly hierarchy in all things, and grace does not come through a downward mystical enlightenment by the ordained but through the sufferings

---

12. Congar, *L'Église de Saint Augustin à l'époque moderne* (Paris: Cerf, 1970), 427.

of Christ, active in sacraments. In different historical times, the one ministry unfolds itself differently, "*in diversis.*"[13]

This theology of the priesthood stands behind the scandals of sexual misconduct in the clergy. The priest is employed and retained as an unclear metaphysical being apart from actual ministry. He is retained as a metaphysical link with God even when he is an ecclesial liability. This third theology has cost a lot of money. The second, the hierarchical, will cost money, too, if it is not modified.

In all three theologies, baptism counts for very little. These theologies are questionable not because theologians do not like them anymore, but because something has been happening in the Church for fifty years to bypass them, bringing to life old and new forms of theology, and therefore ministry, in the Church.

Let us return to the community of the Spirit. Christian structures and rules and beliefs serve the indwelling of the Spirit, which Thomas Aquinas says is the most basic reality in the teaching of Jesus and in the New Covenant.[14] The Spirit brings the baptized to ministerial activities, some transitory, some lasting and important. Today, for many, life in the Spirit is bringing ministry.

This theology of the life and ministry of the baptized from the Spirit is not a radical program. It is a rediscovery of the self-understanding of the Churches after Pentecost. We should heed the words of Saint Paul to the Thessalonians (1 Thessalonians 5:19), the same words Karl Rahner—whose one hundredth birthday we celebrated this year—chose in 1962 for the theme of a first talk on the coming council, Vatican II: "Do not quench the Spirit."

---

13. Thomas Aquinas, *Contra impugnantes Dei cultum et religionem,* c. 4. par. 12; *Summa theologiae* 37, 2; 37, 2, ad 2. Aquinas very carefully calls grace "a bestowed sharing in the divine nature through a kind of participation of likeness" ("communicando consortium divinae naturae per quamdam similitudinis participationem") (*Summa theologiae* I-II, 112, 1).

14. *Summa theologiae* I-II, 106, 1.

6. Lay Ministers and Ordained Ministers

Rev. Michael J. Himes, Boston College

The 1983 Code of Canon Law defines the Christian faithful as those who, inasmuch as they have been incorporated in Christ through baptism, have been constituted as the people of God. For this reason—since they have become sharers in Christ's priestly, prophetic, and royal office in their own manner—they are called to exercise the mission God entrusted the Church to fulfill in the world in accord with the condition proper to each one (Canon 204, 1). The Code of Canon Law then informs us that "By divine institution, there are…in the Church sacred ministers who in law are also called clerics; the other members of the Christian faithful are called lay persons" (Canon 207, 1).

Before turning to the rights and obligations proper to the laity and to the clergy, the Code of Canon Law deals with the rights and duties of all members of the Church, lay and clerical alike. Not only are the members of the Church "free to make known to the pastors of the Church their needs, especially spiritual ones, and their desires" (Canon 212, 2) but, "according to the knowledge, competence, and prestige which they possess, they have the right and even at times the duty to manifest to the sacred pastors their opinion on matters which pertain to the good of the Church and to make their opinion known to the rest of the Christian faithful…" (Canon 212, 3). So laity as well as clergy are not only free, they may be obliged to speak to their pastors and to the community of the faithful at large on matters that pertain to the well-being of the Church.

Forty years after the Second Vatican Council, these canons may not strike us as remarkable. Consider, however, that less than a century and a quarter before the issuance of the 1983 Code, John Henry

Newman was forced to resign the editorship of the journal in which he had advanced the idea that the faithful, in particular the laity, should be consulted in matters of doctrine.[1] The highest-ranking English-speaking member of the Roman curia at the time, Monsignor George Talbot, spoke for many church officials when he dismissed Newman's suggestion as absurd: "What is the province of the laity? To hunt, to shoot, to entertain. These matters they understand, but to meddle with ecclesiastical matters they have no right at all...."[2] Imagine how gratified Cardinal Newman would be and how scandalized Monsignor Talbot after reading the 1983 Code of Canon Law.

Undoubtedly, the theological understanding of the vocation of the laity has developed astonishingly in the last century. The theology of what was called Catholic Action and the groundbreaking work of scholars such as Yves Congar and Henri de Lubac laid the foundation for Vatican II's *Apostolicam Actuositatem,* the Decree on the Apostolate of Lay People. However, the 1983 Code goes past the Vatican II decree in a significant way. Vatican II states, "The characteristic of the lay state being a life led in the midst of the world and of secular affairs, lay people are called by God to make of their apostolate, through the vigor of their christian spirit, a leaven in the world"(section 2). The Decree on the Apostolate of Lay People emphasizes that the focus of the laity's activity is in the world, as contrasted with the clergy's work, which is within the ecclesiastical structure. In short, normally the layperson works in the world and the ordained person works in the Church.

That division of labor seems theologically inadequate and practically unworkable. In the years since Vatican II, the steady decline

---

1. John Henry Newman, *On Consulting the Faithful in Matters of Doctrine,* ed. John Coulson (Kansas City, MO: Sheed and Ward, 1961). Newman originally published the article in the July 1859 issue of *The Rambler.*

2. Ibid., 41.

in numbers of persons active in ordained ministry has reached the point that there is serious question whether the faithful can have access to the sacraments, especially the Eucharist (to which they have a "right," according to Canon 213 of the 1983 Code). The ratio of the total number of diocesan and religious priests to the number of the faithful has dropped by 63 percent worldwide in the thirty years from 1969 through 1999. In the United States, the decline has been 59 percent in the same period. In Europe, the ratio of priests to people fell 22 percent, while Central and South America saw an astonishing 80 percent decline.

Some have tried to take comfort from the 57 percent increase in the number of priests in Africa; however, the number of Catholics in Africa rose by 206 percent between 1969 and 1999, so the ratio of priests to the total Catholic population actually decreased by 149 percent.

In 2000, 471 diocesan priests were ordained in the United States; that same year 778 died and 85 left the active ministry, for a total loss of 392 priests.[3]

On a personal note, I was ordained for the Diocese of Brooklyn, which has the fifth-largest number of Catholics in the country; the next-door Diocese of Rockville Centre is the eighth largest. When I entered the major seminary in 1969, the two dioceses together had over 240 seminarians preparing for ordination; in the 2003-2004 academic year, they had a combined total of fewer than 40. Currently one of seven parishes in the United States has no resident priest; as the large ordination classes of the 1950s and 1960s die or retire, the decline in the number of active ordained priests will actually become steeper.

The primary factor that has prevented this crisis of ordained

---

3. Richard W. Miller, "Introduction," in *The Catholic Church in the 21st Century: Finding Hope for Its Future in the Wisdom of Its Past,* ed. Michael J. Himes (Liguori, MO: Liguori Publications, 2004), x-xi.

ministry from crippling the Church is the increasing number of laypeople actively engaged in ecclesial ministries. At the Long Island seminary at which fewer than 40 men will prepare for ordination to the priesthood next year, over 200 women and men are studying for degrees in theology and ministry.

Nor is this happening on the parish level alone. For example, the active membership of the Catholic Theological Society of America, the professional association of Catholic theologians in the United States and Canada, was over 90 percent male in 1971, and almost all of them were priests. In 1991, the CTSA's active membership was only slightly over 65 percent male, and only half of them were ordained. This means that the teaching of theology in Catholic universities and colleges in the United States and Canada was already predominantly a lay undertaking a dozen years ago.

The trend has, of course, only accelerated in the intervening years. It is now impossible for the Church to function on any level—diocesan or parochial—or in any mission—charitable or educational—without the active engagement of large numbers of laypeople. Thus, for practical reasons it is now impossible to distinguish between the clergy and laity on the basis of spheres of work.

The attempt to make such a distinction is also theologically unsound.[4] In *Lumen Gentium,* the Dogmatic Constitution on the Church, Vatican II teaches that "Though they differ essentially and not only in degree, the common priesthood of the faithful and the ministerial or hierarchical priesthood are none the less interrelated; each in its own way shares in the one priesthood of Christ" (section 10). In the last several decades, this essential difference has been con-

---

4. As a diocesan or secular priest, I have long favored a thorough examination of the differences between the distinctive charisms of the secular priest and the religious priest. I strongly suspect that the results would further support the position outlined here and would undercut the allotment of spheres in which the world is assigned to the laity and the sanctuary to the clergy.

strued in two ways. One has been to invoke the metaphysical language of ontology. Thus, we sometimes hear it said that one is "ontologically changed" by ordination. If one examines this claim, however, either one ends up in conclusions that appear bizarre at best and flatly heretical at worst or one recognizes that the language of ontology is simply employed to underscore that there is a real difference between the ordained and the laity but does not offer much assistance in determining precisely in what that real difference consists.

The other way of trying to frame the distinction between clergy and laity has been functional, that is, the clergy are empowered to perform certain functions that the laity cannot, and it is the performance of those functions that constitutes this difference in essence and not merely in degree of which the Second Vatican Council document speaks. The difficulties with this approach are obvious. First, if the performance of particular functions, such as presiding at Eucharist and extending absolution in the sacrament of reconciliation, were the constitutive difference between the ordained and the laity, it would follow that ceasing to perform those functions would erase the difference. Thus, a person who cannot perform the distinctive tasks of the ordained or who resigns from active ministry would cease to be a priest. This, of course, is contrary to the Church's traditional teaching about the permanence of the character of ordination. Further, it is extremely difficult (I believe impossible) to establish a list of functions that have always and everywhere throughout the history of the Church been the exclusive preserve of the ordained. So it would seem that the functional approach to understanding the distinction between laity and clergy is as unsatisfactory as the "ontological change" approach.

Let me suggest a different way of casting the relationship between laity and clergy, one that is more faithful to the tradition of Catholic life and thought and that better describes our current experience in the Church here and abroad. The distinction between clergy and laity is best understood in terms of a classically Catholic category: sacramentality.

The sacramental principle so central to the Catholic vision holds that what is always and everywhere true must be embodied somewhere, sometime, so that it can be recognized and celebrated. Sacred time and sacred space are examples of this principle. If God is everywhere, we must select somewhere to acknowledge and honor the presence of God. There is nothing intrinsically holier about a church than about a parking lot, a bank, or a supermarket. By consecrating a particular place as a church or chapel, we set aside a space in which we attend to the divine presence.

So, too, all time is God's time. There is nothing intrinsically holier about Sunday than about any other day of the week. But if all time is God's time, then some time we need to notice that fact, to set aside particular times and days and seasons as holy.

Sunday sacramentalizes the holiness of all time; a church or chapel or shrine sacramentalizes the omnipresence of God. This sacramental principle may provide a classically Catholic way of distinguishing the laity and the clergy.

I suggest that there are responsibilities to which the Church is always called at every moment of its existence, whether in the earliest days of the fledgling community in Jerusalem or now as a worldwide communion, and on every level of its life, be it the domestic Church at its most local level, the family, or the Church universal. Many such responsibilities undoubtedly exist at any given time or place, but at least three are always and everywhere part of the Church's mission. One is the responsibility to maintain and build up the unity of the body of Christ, to hold together the local community and foster the communion of all local communities with one another in the universal Church.

The second responsibility is to and for the word of God, by which

I mean Scripture as well as the whole of the Church's reflection on and celebration of the revelation of God normatively expressed in Scripture, what we have often called Tradition. Church Tradition must be explored, explained, and passed to others, especially the next generation.

The third responsibility always and everywhere present in the Church is service to others within and outside the community. Any person or community that claims it has no interest in or sense of responsibility for fostering communion, handing on the word of God, or responding to those in need is clearly not the Church of Christ.

These three responsibilities have classic names: episcopacy, presbyterate or priesthood, and diaconate. The episcopal role in the Church is the building up of the body of Christ by deepening the communion of Christians with one another and the unity of the local communities with one another and with the Church universal. The presbyteral or priestly role is preserving and unfolding Church Tradition in word and worship, and the diaconal role is giving direct service to those in need inside and outside the Christian community.

Who has these three responsibilities? Everyone, by virtue of baptism. We are accustomed to speaking of a universal or common priesthood, a priesthood of all believers. I suggest that there is also an episcopacy of all believers and a diaconate of all believers. Each of us became responsible for the episcopal, presbyteral, and diaconal dimensions of the Church's life when we were baptized. But, in accord with the sacramental principle that so deeply characterizes Catholicism, if by baptism everyone is bishop, priest, and deacon, some persons must publicly embody each of those responsibilities. What is given to all must be sacramentalized by some. That is what ordination does: sets aside some persons to incarnate the episcopal, priestly, or diaconal role to which all are called by baptism.

This inverts the way in which the relation of the laity and clergy used to be cast. In the early and mid twentieth century, the mission of the laity (usually termed "Catholic Action") was described as the extension of the mission of the hierarchy; the laity participated in the mission of the ordained. I suggest that the fundamental episcopacy, priesthood, and diaconate in the Church are conferred on all of us by baptism and that some are called to sacramentalize them by ordination. Baptism is more fundamental than holy orders. What is conferred on all by baptism is sacramentalized in some by orders. The episcopacy, priesthood, and diaconate of the laity are made manifest, are sacramentalized, in the ordained episcopacy, priesthood, and diaconate, which in turn express the episcopacy, priesthood, and diaconate of all of the baptized.

To conclude, let me point out three consequences of this sacramental understanding of the clergy's relationship to the laity. First, it is not only unnecessary, it is impossible to distinguish the laity from the clergy by delineating different spheres in which they work for the gospel, assigning "the church" to the clergy and "the world" to the laity. Second, the ordained ministry exists for the sake of and in service to the ministry of the baptized. Newman answered his bishop's question "Who are the laity?" by commenting that the Church would look foolish without them.[5] Indeed, it would. Saint Thomas famously described a sacrament as that which effects what it signifies.[6] Where there is nothing to signify, there is no effect. If the ministry of the ordained sacramentalizes the ministry of the baptized, then there can be no ministry of the ordained without the ministry of the baptized. Third, the best way to strengthen a sign is to strengthen what it signifies. The best and truest way to affirm and

---

5. Newman, *On Consulting the Faithful in Matters of Doctrine,* 18f.

6. *Summa theologiae,* III, q. 62, a. 1, ad 1 (Leonine ed., 12:20a): "Et inde est quod, sicut communiter dicitur, [sacramenta] efficiunt quod figurant."

support the ministry of the ordained is to affirm and support the ministry of the baptized. Neglect and disparagement of the episcopacy, priesthood, and diaconate of the laity inevitably destroy the episcopacy, priesthood, and diaconate of the clergy.

Let me offer a concluding observation. We are only beginning to appreciate the mission of the laity in the life of the Church. I suspect that, as usual in the Church's history, experience must precede theological clarity. As the laity realize their mission, we will better understand its dimensions and its relation to the role of the clergy. And the theologians who do so will probably be laypeople.

Panel Discussion

Richard Miller: We are unable to treat all of the questions today, so we tried to collate them into certain themes. For the next hour, we will ask questions of the speakers.

The first question is in regard to the signs of the times. What social, cultural, and political conditions shape the Church today? What will historians say of the period in the Church from Vatican II to the present regarding political, social, and cultural events or changes that shaped the Church in the late twentieth century? What has shaped the present-day Church, and what do you think is important in that?

Francine Cardman: I think we are just beginning to see some of the more recent ones, some of the older, obvious ones in the United States: that we are no longer an immigrant Church and no longer economically sort of below middle class, that we are a much more affluent, much more educated, and much more culturally responsive and responsible community. I think that is, in many ways, shaping these movements immediately after Vatican II and this resurgence of laypeople taking responsibility for their own religious life and for the Church. I think a lot of that has to do with the economic and educational and political position of Catholics in the United States. That is one factor.

I think a much larger factor, both in the United States and worldwide, is what Karl Rahner identified as the real globalization of the Church and its mission, in the twentieth century and now into the twenty-first century. With that, and much bigger than that in many ways, is the demographic shift of the Church's center of gravity from the North Atlantic, really, to the Southern Hemisphere, ultimately, and we are also beginning to see the impact of that in the very different and divergent populations in the United States. That is going to change things significantly in ways I don't think we've even begun to imagine. Those are, I think, two of the biggest ones.

I think a third factor might be, and this comes especially out of a North American experience but maybe European and beyond that as well, a growing sense of the social and political value and necessity of participation at every level of human life and a sense that it is not just for outside the Church. It is for inside the Church as well. There is a sense of participation, of ownership, that decisions should be made at the level of the persons and by the people whom those decisions affect, a kind of subsidiarity, a growing sense of a very large chorus of voices and not just a small minority of voices that determine how we live as communities, whether in the Church or in the larger world. That demand for participation, which I think is finally the kind of coming to fruition of values that started in that great/horrible/terrible eighteenth century that ended in the French and American Revolutions, the Enlightenment, and so on; that demand is really coming to maturity. I don't think it will be possible to have a Church for very long that functions without that kind of participation, that kind of subsidiarity, that kind of collegiality, that the social and political experiences of peoples across the world demand.

Kenan Osborne: One thing we would have to add is that the Church has been, for instance, in Kerala, India, for two thousand years. The Church has been in Korea since 1500, and it was run by laypeople until the French missionaries came over. The Church has been in many other places, so if we think in a Euro-American way, we need to talk about a different kind of Church. One thing we will learn is that the Church is a much bigger thing than we ever thought. Who will be active in that kind of Church? We will discover Asian people and African people who are operative and have been operative in the Church whom we don't even know about right now, that they are Church people. Nigerian author Elizabeth Izicar somewhere quotes a fellow also, I believe, from Nagada, Nigeria, who said something like, "The Christians came into Africa and converted us to Christianity in the last three hundred years, and they write the history of the Church. I think we need a new history of the spirit in Africa and it would be written by the Holy Spirit, who has been here for about four thousand years."

Richard Miller: Since you are theologians as well as historians, how do you see the Holy Spirit at work in the history you described? Were there only human forces at work, or are some of the developments the work of the Spirit? If so, which?

Thomas O'Meara: From the perspective of having lived through the post-conciliar period—I was ordained just a few months before Vatican II started—I am a little surprised at the question because it is easier to think that there are supernatural forces at work than it is to think there are human forces. If you take the issue of the emergence of the new world that we were talking about, of lay ministry, that just suddenly occurred. There was no program from the bishops, there was no program from the theologians that said that this is how a diocese and parish should now structure itself. Not at all.

The first example I knew was a Dominican sister in my parish in Madison, Wisconsin, who started a ministry to the sick and aged—she did that, she did a lot of other things, too. She then had about ten people in the parish who helped her in that ministry a few hours a week. Then she had dozens and dozens more people who helped her. That was the first example I ever saw of ministry that was not the sisters in the parochial school and the priests in the church.

You rightly emphasized that the decline in the number of priests was not a factor in the emergence of the laity, and you had that pic-

ture from your age presentation. But if you go back to the very beginning, the first programs in theology for people who were not
seminarians, short-term programs, graduate schools and universities in the seminaries, the sudden multiplication of full-time positions in parishes—that was all in place ten years before there was an
awareness that there was going to be a shortage of priests. *Ten years*
before. The shortage of priests came later. So I don't see how you
explain this enormous change except through the action of the Holy
Spirit. It is different in country after country, but it does exist pretty
much everywhere in the world, and it came out of indigenous and
spontaneous causes. So, I think it is very hard not to think that the
Holy Spirit decided that the original view of the community was to
come back, and the ministry was not to be simply the providence of
a few people. I think, as some others have said today, too, you can
also go back and see that, in the founding of all the religious orders
and movements, in a way the Holy Spirit is always trying to get the
ministry out of being just one form, but in our time it has set this in
motion with tremendous force and change.

Francine Cardman: When I teach Church history, this kind of question comes up all the time, and especially some of early Church history, which is not always edifying. I want to underline Tom's point
that it is much easier to believe it is the work of the Holy Spirit. That
the Church has endured and is still present and still active is a sign
of that in itself but, theologically, the only way the Holy Spirit acts,
the only way God acts, the only way Jesus acts, is through human
agency. That is who we are in the world, and I would like to stop
perpetuating that distinction because it sort of blurs and mystifies
the real meaning of human history, human life, and what living it in
the presence of and for God is about. I would like to underline that
very strongly.

Richard Miller: What principles help indicate the movement of the Spirit through human life to distinguish between false prophets and real prophets, or the true or authentic teaching and false teaching? What principles from the history of the Church allow us to move forward?

Michael Himes: A very broad but very important one would be humanization. Tomorrow we celebrate the feast of the Trinity. One way to recognize the work of the Triune God is through perceiving that God creates us to be something and then is that with us; that is what the Incarnation means, that God has come and lived humanly with us and then makes it possible for us to do what we have just seen God do, that is, the work of the Spirit—that what we are created to be, the Spirit leads us to actually be. So if you want to know the work of the Spirit, anytime anybody is enabled by anyone else or anything else to be more loving, more intelligent, freer, more responsible, more generous, more open, more insightful, more creative, that is the work of the Spirit.

Carolyn Osiek: I have my informal list of criteria for determining true prophecy. One criterion is that the prophet is reluctant to be a prophet—always beware of prophets who are just too eager to be prophets—because the prophetic person knows the cost. The second follows from that: you get mixed reviews. Some people think this conflict is wonderful, and a lot of people think it is not. Real prophecy causes conflict. The third is you never really know until later whether it's true prophecy or not; you only know in retrospect, so you have to take your chances at the moment.

Richard Miller: How is prophecy "still very much alive"? That quote is from your talk.

Carolyn Osiek: The Spirit is very clever and takes forms that will be acceptable in a given society. In the first century in a Christian community, someone would stand up in the assembly say, "Thus says the Holy Spirit," and say something. In the kind of culture in which most of us live, if someone says that, we send them off for a psychiatric evaluation. So, the Spirit takes other forms. One of those forms, I think, is individual prophecy that speaks to the person and comes from unexpected directions. But the other is public prophecy, the figure of the person who takes the unpopular stand which will, in retrospect, turn out to be right. So those are two examples, I think, of the way prophecy functions today. Sometimes it is a public figure, sometimes it is not who the true prophet is, and we can all think of possibilities. I think one clear example is Mother Teresa, I mean that is just very clear. And what is the response to her? "Wow!" and then sort of, "Oh, I couldn't do that," and go home. So, sometimes a public figure points to a need that is not being met. But sometimes it is much quieter, as well. I was doing a workshop on prophecy in West Virginia and was struggling with some questions of my own, and at lunch someone said something to me that really spoke the word. He had no idea he was doing that, and it resolved the thing for me. At the end of the day I said, "I want you to know that you prophesied to me." He didn't miss a beat. He said, "Oh, I know, I get it all the time from my three-year-old."

Richard Miller: Does the Spirit move us to merely reform or to renew ministries from the history of the Church, or does openness to the Spirit call us to consider new forms of ministers and ministries?

Kenan Osborne: If you read Church history, you are going to see that a new ministry starts locally. Then, you know, here's Kansas City, and then Leavenworth says, "Oh, I like that," and maybe Independence says, "I think that's a good thing to do, too." You read that the early Church sort of moved in that interrelational way that was up on the board with all those little circles and lines between them; if it picks up, you begin to develop the idea that, well, this might be a good form of ministry for a larger region. Rarely does it start from the top and come down.

When these things get started, sometimes they are looked upon as, "Well this isn't right." It wasn't always that way. That's tradition, but that doesn't mean it can't change. And then these little changes come up, changes in liturgy, changes in ministry, and so many things happen at a local level and maybe they die out, they served their purpose. But maybe they move on to a little larger thing and spark a movement, and things are established that way. That's why you have to read the signs. And don't cover it over right away just because it's not the way it has always been, whether we stand or kneel, or whatever it might be.

Francine Cardman: History is important, but not just to go back to the past or to reuse it as the sources of renewal or reform in the present, which is one very good use of history. The bigger uses of history are about the dynamics of history, about where change comes from, how it happens, and that it is an open process; it is not finished, it has just started, if you want the first two thousand years for Church. It can be a much longer story before it's over.

I think one of the things we lose sight of is that we want a comprehensible narrative, a story we can understand, and we tell it as a story of organic growth and development, and not as a story of sometimes change and reversal. We have this sort of human penchant for continuity, but I think we also need to be able to see discontinuity in the past, and to be able to envision new things in the future. What is that prophecy of Joel about? "The young shall dream dreams," and so on (Isaiah 40:28-31). It is about change and openness to the future, so to me, the real use of history is about freedom for the future.

So it seems to me that Jesus' ultimate message, "I make all things new"—newness, and openness to that kind of newness, is an essential part of what it is about, trying to be Church wherever one is, whenever one is.

Richard Miller: Can you point to a particular point in Church history when the Church handled a time of transition well? What might we learn from this today in our own time of transition?

Francine Cardman: In the period of the evangelical movements, the transition was handled badly for a century or two, and then there was a moment where someone like Innocent III also saw, "OK, we are going to stop fighting these guys. We need what they have." He says to Francis and Clare and Dominic, "We need this within the Church. We are actually listening to this." You can also read it as co-optation, but that is entirely too cynical, even for me, at that point. There are moments of that, but another key history gives us, and this is what Sister Carolyn was saying about knowing prophecy retrospectively, is patience and tolerance. There are moments when we have managed to do that.

Carolyn Osiek: Way back in the first century, during the shift from the so-called Council of Jerusalem around 49 or 50, from being only within the framework of Judaism to branching out to become a more universal Church, the old did not die without a fight. But they did it, they made the decision and, as Acts tells us, the practice was already there, the reality was there, and then they made the decision, which is what everyone has been saying today—that practice comes before regularization.

Michael Himes: The Catholic or counter-Reformation is another example. Just think of what the Church looked like at the moment the

Reformation began, if we take 1517 and Luther is nailing up the ninety-five theses as an example. Think what it looked like by 1617. It would have been one hundred years. The Council of Trent. The birth of the Jesuits. Teresa of Ávila. John of the Cross. It was not long before Vincent de Paul. This is an extraordinary, incredibly creative, energetic, wise and, in many ways, daring century. We should not eliminate the Catholic counter-Reformation or the Catholic Reformation as a moment of real wisdom and grace in the life of the Church

Francine Cardman: But after botching the first twenty years…

Michael Himes: Yes, well, after botching the first twenty years, but what's twenty years in the life of the Holy Spirit?

Thomas O'Meara: The Church has had a lot of moments of success in these cultural changes, not in all, but in a lot of them. The birth of new religious orders and congregations and spiritualities after the French Revolution quite successfully influenced the emigration of tens of millions of Catholics to the United States. Most of the period from about 600 to 700 up to Vatican II was somewhat the same; the allusion was made to Rahner's view of the World Church and, in that same essay, the view that Catholicism has not changed very much from the first or second century or from the fifth century until Vatican II. There was a sameness to all of this, so what has happened since the council does not quite fit into those 1400 years. That is unsettling. We are not in a period like the thirteenth century, which was quite successful, yet within the framework of what has just gone before. We are in a period that on many levels is really quite new, and that is very challenging.

Richard Miller: How do you think history could be better used and implemented through the ministry of teaching and catechesis?

Carolyn Osiek: First, we have to know the history, and only if the person doing the teaching and catechizing is sure of what we are saying, can you get across to people that things, indeed, have not always been the same, that there is a process involved here, that we are still in process, that what we were taught (if the *we* is my age and the age of most people here) were absolutes really aren't, and that a knowledge of history frees us because we can take what is now and we can imagine what can be, and we can be secure in that without having to feel that we have all the answers.

Francine Cardman: I second that. Going back to the question about what is the work of humans and what is the work of the Holy Spirit, it would be most helpful in very different ways at very different levels of religious education, catechesis, adult Christian education, and spiritual formation, which I think is another crucial, barely started task, to understand that to teach the story of how this whole life of Christianity, of the Church, of Christian faith, has unfolded in history is to make it more concrete, more real, more human, more like our life, more accessible to us, and more understandable and to demystify it. But the whole point of that is greater freedom and greater responsibility and accountability. It is actually something we can be a part of. It is not mysterious, it is not different, it is processes that we are aware of and involved in every day, whether something simple, like that the Bible didn't drop down from heaven or how much we know or don't know about Jesus and the early Church from the witness we have in the Scriptures, or something more complex, like doctrines didn't always exist in their full-blown forms from whenever period they come into being. Learning history with competence and intelligence that students exercise in the rest of their lives is crucially important, whether you are talking about first-graders or people in their nineties, and everybody in between. That is an incredibly important aspect of religious education and spiritual formation in the Church, and I think knowledge of history and of human participation, the utter necessity of human participation in this process, is one important key for doing that.

Richard Miller: Please elaborate on the status and role of women and how they changed in the first millennium. One of the issues is house-churches; were there ever female presiders?

Carolyn Osiek: My next book is on women deacons and presbyters through the year 600. The book after that is going to be on women in house-churches and early Christianity. The ancient Mediterranean society was androcentric, even when people start using the language of equality, which was rare, and they never talked about equality between men and women. The stoics, who were the rare exception, asked the question, "Do women have the same capacity for virtue as men?" And they said yes. However, the ways they are supposed to live it out are entirely different. So you are dealing with a society that had not been through the Enlightenment in terms of that whole understanding of human nature.

Be that as it may, we have certainly some good evidence that, by the year 80, in the parts of the society that were influenced by Roman culture, definite advances had been made in the social freedom and power of women. Meanwhile, on the eastern side of the Mediterranean comes the rise of Christianity, and it seems as if the early Christians bought into the Roman attitude toward women to a certain extent, given that the example of what was preserved of Jesus gives no negative examples. And that is fascinating, because at the same time that you have the writing of what we call the "household codes," with the submissive patterns, you also have the writing of the gospels. The two are very different in that sense, with the household codes simply repeating the common understanding, not being particularly repressive, and certainly inasmuch as that movement was happening and Christians were part of that, there were new opportunities for leadership for women.

As for women presiding in house-churches, we see that in Colossians 4:15—it talks about Nympha and the ecclesia in her house, the church in her house. In Acts 12:12, Mary, the mother of John Mark, has a gathering at her house, which presumably is also a house-church. Probably some examples are in the letters of Ignatius of Antioch. And did these people then preside at the meal? That would be the normal conclusion.

One of the things I am really working on hard in the non-Christian sources is trying to find what people say about women running households, and it is hard to find. We know that there were women who ran households, but it was not the norm. So there is no idealizing discussion about it; you have to really read between the lines. But there is evidence for it: when a Christian woman is running a household, and she has a meeting of the church in her house, the person whose house you're in is the patron of the group and, therefore, the normal presider at the meal. In those first centuries, the sensitive issue was not who did the prayer over the bread and wine; it was who had the right teaching. In many cases, the teacher may not necessarily have been the patron and the presider at the meal. There might have been a specialist who was the teacher and the propounder of Scripture, because at the symposium at the later part of the meal, when you got into the discussion and the prayer, the host did not have to lead, anybody could. But at the meal, the person in whose house you were was the leader, so that gives us our answer to that question.

Richard Miller: Why did you separate the material into two books? It sounds like the material goes together.

Carolyn Osiek: No, in fact, it doesn't go together. The deacon/presbyter material is much later. You've got Phoebe the deacon and then you have Pliny, but then it moves into the third century, so most of the material is in the 300s through 600, and that is a collection of sources, whereas the women in house-churches is first century, first and early second.

Richard Miller: One of the issues then becomes how and why and when did some laypeople get chosen to be priests?

Francine Cardman: That's another one I don't think we can put a date or a specific moment of process on. One of the things that is so interesting about this early history is that so much of the stuff we take as normative has no identifiable local authority and certainly no centralized process for authorizing it. It just happened, and it took hold, and it spread in the ways that Kenan was talking about earlier for later centuries. Earlier, we talked about Ignatius of Antioch, saying he was precocious in his promotion of bishops, presbyters, and deacons as "this is the ideal pattern of ministry," which took almost that entire second century to get a good foothold, and it took another good fifty or sixty years to spread significantly. Whenever the *Didaskalia* was written, maybe sometime around 200 to 230, they were still arguing about why and how laypeople should respect their bishops and the presbyters and the deacons and so on, setting out lines of authority and such. But certainly by around 200 we have the Hippolytus apostolic tradition, which gives us liturgical rites for the ordination of bishops, presbyters, and deacons and points out that widows are installed but not ordained and that virgins are simply recognized as having made a personal choice. So you are beginning to get something, whatever this is, bishops, presbyters, and deacons with specific rites of ordination around 200 and then later on, and you see it in the *Didaskalia*. The theology of it continues to evolve, as is the practice, but sometime between 200 and 250, you can really point to that and identify it.

Carolyn Osiek: The language of priesthood goes with the idea that Christians are replacing the temple. It is first applied to the bishop because when they begin, Paul already says this is the real covenant, but to say that it is the new covenant, it is the new temple, it is the new Israel—when that idea sets in, you begin to get the language of temple, stronger language of sacrifice, and the language of priesthood.

Richard Miller: Changing here a bit, these questions are for Dr. Gaillardetz. Given that the Church has no structures in which laypersons can influence change, how do you see your proposals being implemented? Do you have specific suggestions for the United States Catholic Conference of Bishops Subcommittee for beginning work on your second modest proposal?

Richard Gaillardetz: There is a lot more work to be done in terms of securing structures that would allow input from the laity, but it is not completely true that those structures don't exist now. The Code of Canon Law actually provides a number of opportunities for the laity to participate more than we do in decision-making, not only in terms of diocesan pastoral councils and diocesan synods and plenary councils—the Code of Canon Law allows lay participation in all of those, unfortunately, only consultative participation, but participation nevertheless. As a first step, I encourage dioceses to make fuller use of the structures already present in the Code of Canon Law. So, for example, when diocesan synods have been done well (and they are not always done well), they have been very powerful agents for transformation and renewal in dioceses; many laypeople have felt empowered because their voices and pastoral concerns were heard. I have been involved in several diocesan synodal processes and am impressed with the way that can be done. We need further revisions that would give the laity not only a consultative but a deliberative role in certain Church decisions. There is ample historical precedent for that, but simply a fuller use of the things that are already available to us would go well.

Just as important as the question of institutional structures for the voice of the laity in Church decision-making is a change in consciousness of the kind of that Michael was talking about when he cited the Code of Canon Law, that whole consciousness that the Christian faithful are full members of the Church, that they have a right and an obligation to make their voices heard, their concerns heard. *Lumen Gentium* article 37 talks about the obligation of the laity to voice their concerns to their pastors. Unfortunately, among many of our Church leaders consultation is a nicety, something that is good for bishops to do but is not really integral to the ministry. That whole mindset has to be changed. There has to be a transformation or understanding that teachers can't teach unless they are first learners and that they must learn from inside the whole people of God, so there is a whole consciousness of the Church as corporately a community of discernment and conversation has to be deepened in the life of the Church. Without that, you just go through the motions. You have pastoral councils that are *pro forma* things in which no real conversation takes place. A change in consciousness in the Church still needs to be made, particularly among Church leaders in that regard.

Richard Miller: Father Himes, please give practical ways to strengthen the sign by strengthening what it signifies. What would it look like?

Michael Himes: Let me answer that question in just one or two ways, starting with something Rick Gaillardetz said about the question of what we look for in ordination candidates. One thing I would want to see in a candidate for the office of presbyter is somebody who already exercises presbyteral ministry in a vital and important and successful and powerful way. I don't think you ordain someone and suddenly they are empowered to perform a ministry. What has happened is, they are so manifestly good at this ministry that of course you ordain them as a sacrament of it. That goes back to the example of my friend, Ed Cummings. It is because he is so manifestly a good deacon that you ordain him a deacon! What you don't do is say, "Well, here's somebody who has never done a whit of diaconate in his life. Let's ordain him, and he can start tomorrow." If somebody has no clue as to what the Tradition of the Church is about on Saturday and you ordain him on Sunday, on Monday you will have an ordained boob, not somebody who is miraculously endowed with the capacity to embody and communicate the Tradition. The same is true for bishops and deacons or anyone else. We must recognize that we are drawing people into ordained ministry who have already manifested their strengths, their abilities, their talents, their energies, in that ministry as part of the role of the baptized.

This might mean we ordain people later than we have at many times in the past. We look for somebody who is already manifestly priestly before we ordain him a priest. That we look for somebody who is wonderfully, obviously episcopal before we make him a bishop, just as we look for somebody who is manifestly diaconal before we ordain him as a deacon. The relationship between ordained ministry and the ministry of the baptized has to alter; it has to be changed in lots of ways.

Secondly, there are countries in South America, in Latin America, and especially in Central America, that have begun to experience a slight rise in the number of people seeking ordination. It is very interesting that many of those people come from families in which one or both parents were catechists or ministers at their local communities. The people who come from families of vibrant baptismal ministry find themselves called and desirous to enter into a sacramentalization of those ministries. People who come out of those types of communities understand the value of that ministry and wish to embrace it and be sacramentalized with it by ordination. It is another demonstration of my fundamental point: You strengthen the sign by strengthening that which it signifies.

Richard Gaillardetz: I agree with Michael completely. I think, however, that his principle that you recognize the charism already present and then you ordain the person has implications as well for lay ministry. In the flourishing of lay ministry, sometimes we have forgotten this insight and have confused ministry for volunteerism. I think of the number of parishes that have ministry Sunday once a year where everybody signs up to be a catechist or a lector or whatever it is, and we take all comers. If you are the director of a Christian formation program, the Sunday before your program is supposed to start, you're twisting arms, you're guilting parents, you're doing whatever you can to get those last few catechists. We are a long way from the idea that those are ministries that ought to be charisms, calling people who we think might have a charism for catechesis or for proclaiming the word of God in the liturgy, and we succumb to a kind of crass volunteerism. I think that is a real problem at the level of lay ministry, as well.

It is a problem because, as Michael suggests, until you become the kind of community that is involved and interactive and whose members know one another well enough that those charisms are manifest to one another, so that we can say, "John would be a wonderful catechist, it's so obvious to us," we are going to continue to struggle with this problem. But my point is, it's an issue for ministry in general, not just ordained ministry.

Richard Miller: How would you implement looking for charisms to priesthood among current seminarians?

Richard Gaillardetz: You know what? I'd tear down the seminary. I honestly believe that the Church is going to have to start seriously looking at the wisdom of the whole model of forming people for ordination to the presbyterate by locking them away in a monastic-style facility for five years. [Applause.] Formation work has advanced over the last few years. For example, a lot of formation programs do very good jobs with pastoral years and so forth which, in fact, are more or less the way the entire seminary process should be structured. My view is that seminarians ought to spend their entire time in a parish community, taking courses much the way a lot of people in this room take courses while doing and negotiating other things and constantly having their work and their new insights tested among the people of God. Yeah, that is pretty radical. By the way, it is an experiment that was tried in Brazil before the Vatican put the nix on it, but I think it will take nothing less radical than that to reflect the kind of changes that we are talking about.

Richard Miller: Father Himes, what is the relationship between bishops, priests, deacons, and laity?

Michael Himes: One thing I think has happened over the last thirty years in the Church is that, by and large, the morale of our diocesan clergy is not good and, by the way, I entirely endorse what Rick Gaillardetz just said about seminaries. I think morale is much better among priests in religious communities than among diocesan clergy, secular clergy, for a number of reasons. One is that priests in parish ministry are called upon to be jacks-of-all-trades ministerially. This is a broad and sweeping generalization, but I will say it for the sake of saving some time. One thing that has concerned me for some time is that seminaries are doing a good job of educating their seminarians for ordination; we train people to be presbyters and then ordain them and tell them to spend the rest of their lives as bishops and deacons. That, in fact, we train people to be responsible to and knowledgeable of the Tradition, if their education works. That's what we try to turn out. But then we tell people that when you go into the parish, you are going to spend most of your time as a type of community leader, which is a much more episcopal role, and an overseer and administrator of charity and finances, a much more diaconal role. So we ordain people to the presbyterate but then want them to live as bishops and deacons, so you have an all-purpose ministry that nobody has ever been expected to perform in the life of the Church. It is the reason, in my observation, and I really feel passionate about this, that most of the best diocesan priests I know go to bed every night discouraged because there are fifty things they were supposed to get done that day and no matter how hard they work and no matter how long they work, they only got through thirty of them. So they go to bed every night saying, "I failed again today." You cannot ask people to live like that, and you certainly can't ask people to live like that and live as celibate at the same time. It is a psychological brutalization of the diocesan priest.

So I think there are real issues about sorting out roles among bishop, priest, and deacon—it is going to take a little time, but I think it has to be done—and consequently you increasingly find pastors who feel trapped between their bishop and the lay parishioners. They know what the laity want to be, they know what the bishop is telling them they have to be able to report back to Rome about. So they try to do enough to keep the laity coming to church and enough to keep the bishop happy and off their backs, and they satisfy no one, including themselves. That is a miserable way to live a life. I really think there needs to be a great deal of sorting out for the psychological health of the diocesan priesthood at the present time.

Richard Miller: The final question is for Father Osborne and the rest of the panel. What does evangelization look like today for the Church?

Kenan Osborne: Ladies and gentlemen, we are on a roll with evangelization, and we have hardly mentioned it here. There are no words in an Asian language for *being*. Your whole ontological thing goes down the tubes. There is no similar word in an Asian language for what we mean by *person*. In our Berkeley area, we have so many Asian students. I tell them this: "Go home and think this through in a Korean way. Go home and think this through in one of the forms of an Indian way. Go home and think this through in a Chinese way, a Filipino way." The whole theology of evangelization will change when it gets into a different thought pattern. That's going to depend on how people look at persons; the relational aspect of who the leader is in the middle of Tibet is a lot different from what it is in the middle of the Congo. The people are going to think about it differently. The sacraments will speak differently. This is a widening of what evangelization means, because you have to take the gospel and translate it into a language that is not Hebrew, Aramaic, Greek, English, German, French, or whatever; it is going to be in another language and it is going to be different. I am so excited about this because I think we who are sitting here in the middle of the United States right now are going to be learning things about what the gospel says in ways we never heard them before.

Richard Miller: That concludes our conference for today. I think all of you will agree with me the need for and importance of communal discussions like this. I thank Bishop Boland for all his support. Without him, this would not be possible. Thank you all very much.

Appendix I

A Sampling of Questions Presented at the Symposium

I. Questions for Sr. Carolyn Osiek, R.S.C.J.

1. Any traces of influences of the "other apostles" besides Peter and Paul?
2. How do you think, through the ministries of teaching and catechesis, that history could better be used?
3. You mentioned presiding, teaching, and service as forms of ministry. Can you speak about their connection with the development of spirituality?
4. What can we learn from the "patronage" experience of the early Church? What are positive and negative implications for current Church experience?
5. How is prophecy still "very much alive"?
6. Were there ever female presiders in house-churches?
7. Is there anything in the New Testament that would prevent the Church from ordaining women as priests?
8. Were the Montanists' charismatic groups assimilated into the Church?

II. Questions for Dr. Francine Cardman

1. How did these influential women like Clothilde themselves become familiar with Christianity?
2. What happened to the deaconesses?
3. How did the laity participate in the selection of their Church leaders?
4. In the early centuries, did anyone ask how Jesus would look upon the developments of authority and power?

5. How and why were some laypeople chosen to be priests?
6. What is the timeline for the development of seminaries and education formation of clergy and its effect on the development of the Church along the way?
7   When and how did our Church's peculiar and fearful attitude about sex originate—coloring the attitudes towards women as being less holy?
8. Since you are a theologian as well as an historian, how do you see the Holy Spirit at work in the history you described?
9. Can you mention the import of Irish monasticism and missionary influence on the West?
10. What are the social, cultural, and political conditions shaping the Church today?
11. What will historians say of the post-Vatican II to the present period of the Church regarding political, social, and cultural currents that shaped the Church?

III. Questions for Rev. Kenan Osborne, O.F.M.

1. Please elaborate on your comment regarding medieval salvation, circa 1000, that "salvation is only for the clergy and monks."
2. Were popes married in these earlier centuries?
3. Were women at the Council of Lateran?
4. Today's laity have access to many forms of communication. Is there a sense that they are truly listened to effectively by the Church structure?
5. What would you say about Opus Dei as a lay reform movement?
6. Do you see history as mostly evolution or devolution?
7. Would you please briefly describe the central ideas of these three theological Traditions (Augustinian, Franciscan, Thomistic)? Are new major Traditions developing?
8. I would like to belong to a group that imitates the house-churches of the early Church. Are there such communities?

9. How do the current sex-abuse issues fit into the historical picture of the Church?

10. Is there a precedent for denying Communion to a person who votes a certain way? How would anyone know how I vote?

11. As laity, our morale is down; we are excluded, scolded, belittled, and not spiritually nourished. How do we live healthily within this present dark milieu of control, clericalism, and conservative judgments within our Church?

IV. Questions for Dr. Richard Gaillardetz

1. How does the Church in the United States gather to consider decisions on the sacredness and dignity of life and reception of the Eucharist?

2. Is it wise to ground a theology of ministry in a liturgical vision of the Church when so many communities, especially in the Third World, lack a presider and have to adapt accordingly?

3. What positive construct exists in the Church today to call forth the discernments that you refer to in your talk?

4. Is not "lay ecclesial ministry" only another step in the hierarchical ladder, creating more separation rather than establishing one body? I submit we are all a priestly people inflamed by the same Spirit. As you said, "Let us not dwell on our impediments, but on all of our charisms."

5. What ministry, if any, do the people in the pew exercise in the liturgy?

6. How would you implement looking for charisms to priesthood among current seminarians? Or how would going to seminary without guarantee of ordination work?

7. Since there are no structures in the Church whereby laypersons can have influence for implementing change, how do you see your proposals being implemented?

8. Regarding your proposal of ritualizing installation of lay minis-

ters, in the 1970s and 1980s there was Catechetical Sunday, when religion teachers were commissioned at Sunday liturgy. What happened to this tradition?

9. In the light of the state of the global Church is it not likely that Vatican III will be a return to Trent rather than a completion of Vatican II?

10. Nice proposals! Do you think they will ever happen?

V. Questions for Rev. Thomas F. O'Meara, O.P.

1. Does the theology of the indwelling of the Spirit presume some sort of formation or baptism alone? Do questions about formation threaten to extinguish the Spirit?

2. Regarding your three theologies "that occlude the life of the Spirit"—I did not hear in any of these an allusion to a "theology of silencing." Is the ban on discussion of women's gifts of leadership in the Church part of the theology that "occludes"?

3. Is the Church authority moving toward a new theology at baptism today?

4. Is baptism not the sign that one has received the Spirit? All are created in the image and likeness of God, therefore do not all have God's Spirit?

5. Would it not serve the Spirit better to go to smaller community Masses instead of our new "megachurches"? How can we do this without allowing the nonordained to "say Mass" and "give Communion" like in the first-century Church?

6. With the emphasis on the connection between baptism and mission in mind; why do we hold infant baptism to be so important? Why not baptism at an age when choice to accept mission can be made?

7. Would you call a baptized Christian's life work "ministry"?

VI. Questions for Rev. Michael J. Himes

1. As you outline the responsibilities of episcopacy, presbyterate, and diaconate, women in today's Church are still excluded from leadership. What does one say to women who have the gifts to share in leadership?

2. Please give practical ways to strengthen the sign by strengthening what it signifies. What would it look like?

3. Are the lay members of the CTSA not soaked in the Tradition? What does their reality say to your framework of ordained ministry?

4. The ministry of the baptized has developed or renewed itself greatly in the last twenty years. Would this not indicate that the ministry of the ordained has done well?

5. What do you do when a bishop, priest, or deacon fails to be that sacramental presence in the community?

6. I believe that the numbers and average age of professional lay ministers points to a coming crisis for lay ministry similar to the crisis now facing the ordained ministry. What can we do to bring forth more ministers?

7. As long as canon law limits ordination to males who are among the baptized, how will baptized women be welcomed to ordination?

8. Please talk about the possibility of gay sacrament of love in the future of the Church.

9. Does our responsibility to the Church end with direct service? What about social justice?

VII. General Questions

1. Can you point to a particular period in Church history when the Church was in a time of transition and it handled the transition well? What might we learn from this today in our time of transition?

2. Does the Spirit move us merely to reform or renew ministries from the history of the Church, or does the Spirit call us to consider new forms of ministries?

3. Please elaborate on the status and role of women and how they changed in the first millennium.

4. What does evangelization look like today for the Church?

5. You have used the term "bishop" often. What kind of preparation did they receive to exercise the authority and power of office?

6. How would you respond to those who say God's revelation does not continue through human experience?

7. As the division grows between the "right" and "left" in the Church and society, what steps do you see emerging toward reconciliation and unity?

Appendix II

Speakers' Biographies

Sr. Carolyn Osiek, R.S.C.J.

Sr. Osiek received degrees from Fontbonne College, Manhattanville College, and Harvard University, where she received her Th.D. She is currently Professor of New Testament at Brite Divinity School, Texas Christian University, in Fort Worth, Texas, having taught for many years at Catholic Theological Union in Chicago. Sr. Osiek has served as president of the Catholic Biblical Association and the Society of Biblical Literature. She is the author of nine books and twenty-seven articles on Scripture.

Dr. Francine Cardman

Dr. Cardman is Associate Professor of Historical Theology and Church History at Weston Jesuit School of Theology in Cambridge, Massachusetts. Dr. Cardman has written widely in her area of expertise. She travels and speaks extensively. Recently she was awarded the Henry Luce Fellowship in Theology to research *Early Christian Ethics: Foundations and Frameworks.*

Rev. Kenan Osborne, O.F.M.

Fr. Osborne is Professor of Systematic Theology, Emeritus, at the Franciscan School of Theology in Berkeley, California. He has mentored hundreds of scholars through their master's degrees and doctoral studies, preparing them for Church service. He has served his religious community in leadership both nationally and internationally, written twelve books, and led major Catholic theological organizations.

Dr. Richard Gaillardetz

Dr. Gaillardetz is the Margaret and Thomas Murray and James J. Bacik Professor of Catholic Studies at the University of Toledo in Toledo, Ohio. He is an official delegate on the U. S. Catholic-Methodist Ecumenical Dialogue and a theological consultant for several committees of the U. S. Conference of Catholic Bishops. In 2000, he received the Sophia Award from the faculty of the Washington Theological Union in recognition of "theological excellence in service to ministry. " A popular lecturer, Dr. Gaillardetz has written extensively, including his recent publication from Liturgical Press, *By What Authority*.

Rev. Thomas F. O'Meara, O.P.

Fr. O'Meara is the William K. Warren Professor of Theology Emeritus at the University of Notre Dame. He has been past president of the Catholic Theological Society of America and in 1991 was awarded the prestigious "John Courtney Murray Award" by the Catholic Theological Society of America. Among his numerous articles and twelve books are his most recent books, *A Theologian's Journey* (2002), *Erich Przywara, S.J., His Theology and His World* (2002), and *Theology of Ministry* (1999).

Rev. Michael J. Himes

Fr. Himes is Professor of Theology at Boston College. His books include *Fullness of Faith: The Public Significance of Theology,* which he coauthored with his brother, Fr. Kenneth Himes, O.F.M., and which was awarded the Catholic Press Association Book Award in 1994; *Doing the Truth in Love: Conversations about God, Relationships and Service;* and *Ongoing Incarnation: Johann Adam Möhler and the Beginnings of Modern Ecclesiology,* which received the Catholic Press Association Book Award in 1998. He has also written several popular video series: *The Mystery of Faith: An Introduction to Catholicism* (10 videotapes, 1994); *Questions of the Soul* (5 videotapes, 1996); *The Vision of the Gospels* (4 videotapes, 2001); and *The Vision of Vatican II for Today* (5 videotapes, 2002).